"Say the prayer and bake the cake. Both are good for your soul. Everything will be alright in the end. If it's not alright, it's not the end."

— *Kathy*

Kathy's
CAKE BOOK

HANNAH HOUSE
PUBLISHING

Copyright © 2020 Kathy Crabb Hannah

All rights reserved.

This book is dedicated
to my little Momma.

I miss her.

Kathy's Cake Book

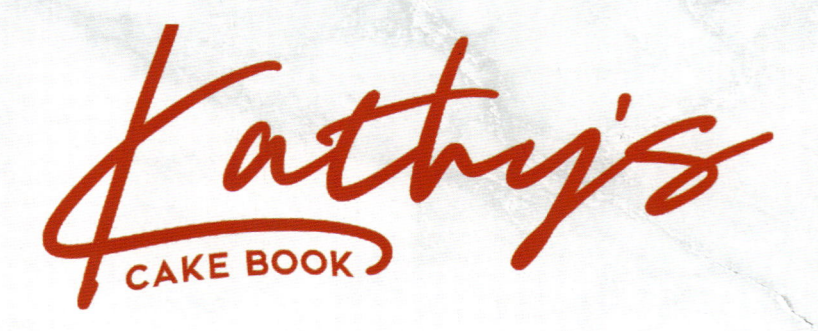

When my family and friends encouraged me to put this little book together, I knew it would be a mash-up of recipes, stories, pictures, and Jesus ideology. That makes editors explode. It makes publishers explode. So, once again. I am self-publishing, self-editing, and giving you my life in the rawest form that's legal! HA!

I have enjoyed pulling the big group of girls in: My daughters, daughters-in-law, granddaughters, and the two little great-granddaughters. They are a group of beautiful and caring girls. We're a family that's largely comprised of women. The age span in the immediate family is about sixty years, between the youngest, Elliana, and myself. She's three, and I'm headed for that BIG sixty-five. The joy has been refreshing, as I've watched them play in icing, pander to the camera, and have food fights in the yard. It's been fun. I appreciate my family more than I could begin to express in writing. I am truly blessed.

And of course, I didn't completely leave the boys out!! Ha!! They're pretty awesome too.

I want to confess up front, not every cake I made was pretty!! But every cake was delicious. Baking is a bit like life, we expect the exterior to dictate the quality at times. That's not the way this thing works. So don't be too hard on yourself when your cake is not perfect, just close your eyes and enjoy the sweetness of the taste. Yes, baking is very similar to life. Enjoy EVERY SINGLE MOMENT. For the cake will be gone one day, and we will be sad we were too busy to truly taste it. Some of us are down to the last piece, and I suggest we make the effort to enjoy each and every bite!!

I pray we learn to bake a bit more love into our cakes, as well as our lives. I will forevermore believe that a three hour conversation around a kitchen table, with cool heads and a piece of chocolate cake, could be the forum to solve the world's problems. Food brings us together. The one thing that's common to all of God's children, no matter the color or political affiliation? Food. We all love food. It's truly an overlooked weapon of peace.

Happy Baking!! Bake it and they will come!!

Photography: Mike Bowling
Graphic Design: Lucretia Kittinger
Recipe Co-Ordinator: Krystal Lawing
Art Director: Eden McCorkle
Hair and make-up: Hope Bowling

Thank you to:
Those of you who allowed me to use your cherished recipes. I love each of you!

the Cake Eaters

Me and Steve

Krystal & Family
Back Row: Krystal, Cameron, Eden
Front Row: Sophie, Brian

Jason & Family
Jason, Emma, Ashleigh, Shellye

Kelly & Family
Mike, Katelanne, Kelly, Hope, Gracie

Adam & Family
Charlee, Grayson, Kaitlyn, Adam, Hannah, Ethan

Aaron & Family
Eva, Ean, Eda, Amanda, Aaron, Eli

Terah & Family
Jon, Logan, Terah

Eden & Family
(Krystal's Oldest Daughter)
Brad, Addi, Eden, & Elli (in front)

Cameron & Dillon
(Krystal's Middle Daughter)

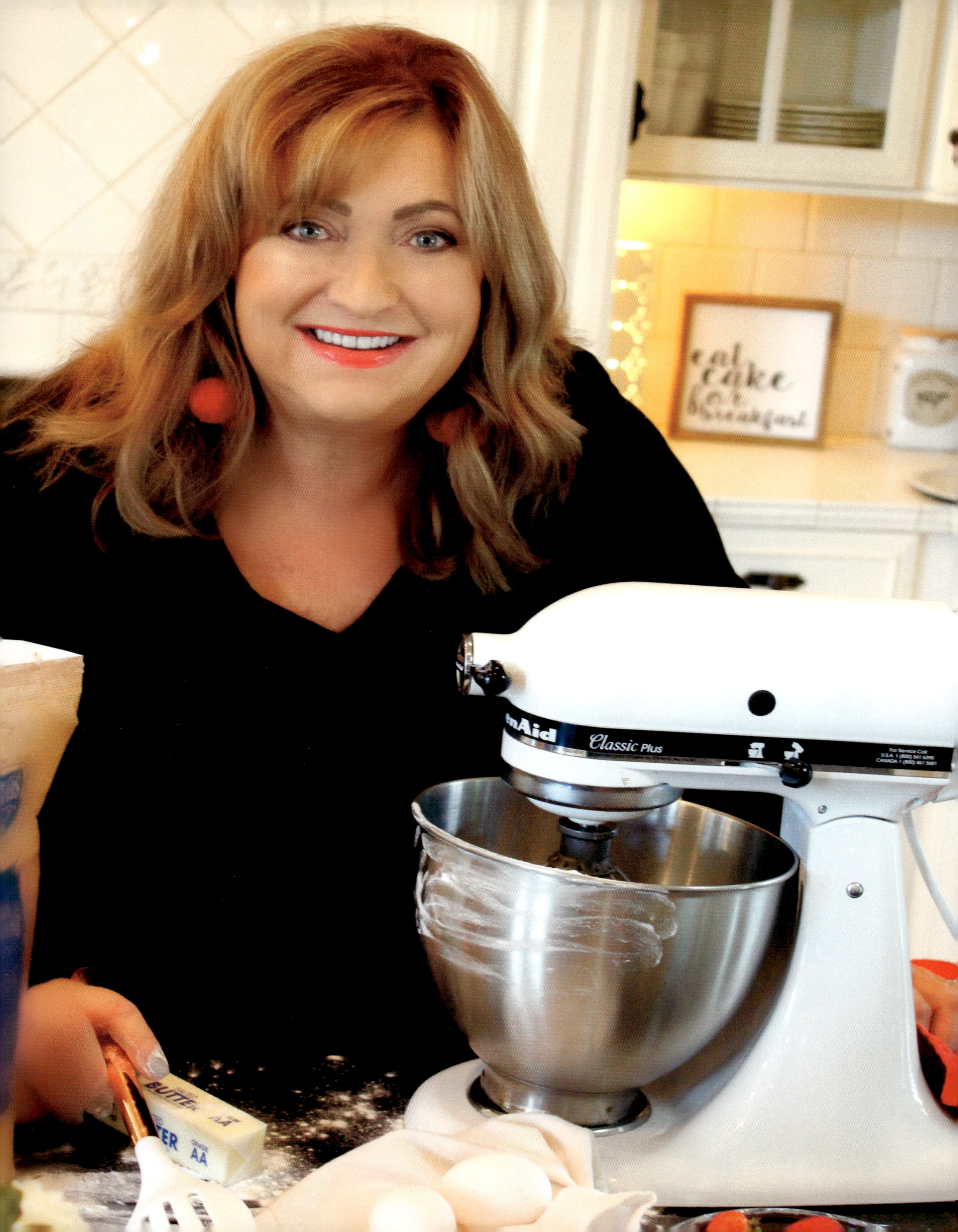
eat cake for breakfast
Classic Plus

Table of Contents

Page 08	Winter
Page 10	Momma's Banana Cake
Page 12	Christmas Chocolate Mint Cake
Page 14	Mike's Bahamian Rum Cake
Page 16	Hot Chocolate Cake
Page 18	German Chocolate Cake
Page 20	Kentucky's Best Jam Cake
Page 22	Anneta's Carrot Cake
Page 24	Perfect Pound Cake
Page 26	Classic Yellow Cake With Chocolate Frosting
Page 28	Friday Night Cupcakes
Page 30	Steve's Hot Peppercorn Cake
Page 32	Spring
Page 34	Best Friend Coconut Cake
Page 36	The Crabb-Turtle Cheesecake
Page 38	Cake For Breakfast Oatmeal Cake
Page 40	Kathy's Pineapple Upside Down Cake
Page 42	Sunday In The South Cherry Pineapple Dump Cake
Page 44	Adam's Anything But Basic White Cake
Page 46	Southern Italian Cream Cake
Page 48	Jason's Favorite Cheesecake
Page 50	Kathy's Sweet Potato Wedding Cake
Page 52	The Peace Cake
Page 54	The Hannah Smorgastarta
Page 56	Summer
Page 58	Banana Split Cake
Page 60	Strawberry Cake
Page 62	The Happy Cake
Page 64	Goldie's Sunshine Cake
Page 66	Oreo Ice Cream Cake
Page 68	Republican Red Velvet Cake
Page 70	Momma's 7UP Cake
Page 72	Pistachio Heaven Cake
Page 74	Luscious Lemon Cake
Page 76	Southern Strawberry Shortcake
Page 78	Jon's Crab Cakes
Page 80	Autumn
Page 82	Aunt Net's October Cake
Page 84	Betty's Famous Sheet Cake
Page 86	Clara's California Orange Cake
Page 88	Sugar And Spice Applesauce Cake
Page 90	Aaron's Caramel Cake
Page 92	Brothers Forever Chocolate Chip Pound Cake
Page 94	Perfect Peanut Butter Cake
Page 96	Chocolate Skillet Cake
Page 98	Three Strands Ultimate Chocolate Cake
Page 100	The Humble Potato Cake
Page 102	Brian's Amazing Eclair Cake
Page 104	Notes

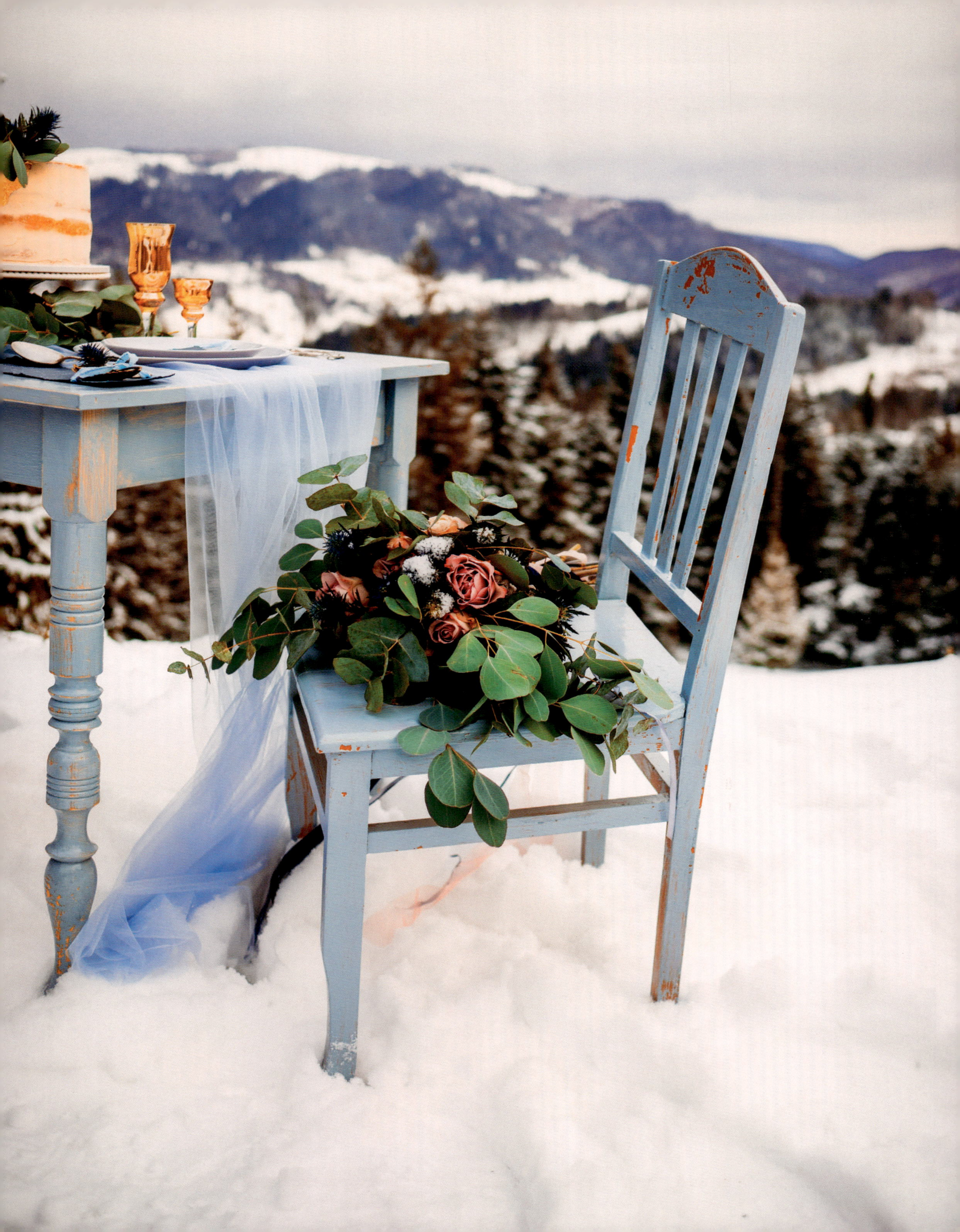

Winter

In the wintertime it's as if you can visually see the bones of the earth. She's a bit naked, a bit humble in appearance. And this look is almost daunting when you look at a mountain. We go to the mountains in the winter, not the summer. We shoot for those Monday through Thursday stays in January, when the chances of snow are high, and the chances of hot chocolate and cake are higher!!

In the winter the mountains seem to be standing and waiting. You know, the same way WE must do at times: Standing, waiting, for the CHANGE to come. Somehow, life happened, and we found ourselves in trouble. The brittleness of the freezing winter air numbed us. We prayed for this BITTER season to pass quick, wishing we could be like a big Momma black-bear and just SLEEP through it. It began with the chilling knock on the door, the call that took your breath and life away, the solemn faced doctor as he began to tell you….the results of "that" report. And you didn't know that you would be in "that" club, ever: The grief club, the abandoned club, the abused club, the sick club. Your life went from July 4th, to January 20th, in ten seconds. From sunshine to bitter cold in less time than it takes to crack an egg. Everything changed.

Every morsel of you died. Your winter appeared, without the normal in order transition that would have been mannerly. But listen up. Winter ain't mannerly. She's cruel, she's cold, and she's long. She leaves us with something no other season does.

Determination.

And her most appealing kindness? She is generous with chocolate. This is where the phrase "Life is short, eat the cake" appropriately fits in this book. If you're in a winter season of life? Take it from the QUEEN of winter and the QUEEN of cake. Part of self-care is eating chocolate!! Ha!!

All kidding aside. As the snow reminds us of the glory of God, the winter moments…as cold as they may be, reveal the beauty of who God really is, and how faithful HE is!!

MOMMA'S BANANA CAKE

This cake is a fabulous way to use those dark, almost ruined bananas!!!
And it's SO GOOD!!

INGREDIENTS

For the CAKE, you will need:
- 3 eggs
- 2 1/2 cups of sugar
- ¾ cup of buttermilk
- ½ tablespoon soda
- ½ tablespoon coconut flavoring
- 4 ripe bananas, crushed
- 2 ½ cups self rising flour
- ¾ cup cooking oil

For the ICING, you will need:
- 1 bag powdered sugar (2 lbs.)
- 1 teaspoon vanilla
- 1 8 oz. package of cream cheese
- ¾ cup brown sugar

You MAY need:
- 1 banana sliced
- ½ cup whole or chopped pecans

STEPS TO COOK

01. Preheat oven to 350 degrees.
02. Beat eggs, sugar, and oil until smooth. Crush your bananas into the mix, the riper the better. Next, add your coconut and buttermilk, soda, and then your flour.

Blend until smooth, but don't over mix the batter.

SUGGESTED PAN SIZE:
- Momma always made three 8" cakes, which allowed for a little more icing. A three layer cake is going to have an extra layer of icing, of course. I think two 10" pans is my preference. But either will work. If it's a lazy day and you only want to deal with one pan? Use a 9" by 13" or a bundt pan.
- If you do the 8" pans, bake for 25 to 35 minutes. You know your oven. But as always, watch it closely.
- If you use the 10" pans, bundt, or a 10" by 13" pan, bake for 35 to 40 minutes. Again, you know your oven. I always coat my pan with cold butter before pouring batter.

TO BLEND THE ICING:
01. Soften cream cheese, blend all ingredients until spreadable. As always with cream cheese icing: if it's too thick? Thin with warm butter, one teaspoon at a time. A little bit goes a long way with powdered sugar.
02. Apply icing between layers while cakes are moderately warm. If you enjoy the icing that runs rather than stays, the drizzled cake presentation, you can ice it all while it's warm.

If you make the bundt, ice while warm.

However, momma always allowed the top and sides to cool so that her icing would be pretty. When you are finished icing the cake, slice that last banana and layer it on top if you plan to consume day of baking. Otherwise, they will turn brown. Use the pecans as a garnish on top if you like. Momma did it both ways. My family will throw a pecan away in a heartbeat, so I don't bother with them unless it's for a photo. Ha-ha!!.

This cake feels like a piece of my life!! Enjoy!!

Anyone who knew my momma, probably remembers that this cake was her "go to" for birthdays. She considered it one of her gifts to her friends and family. Mom lived next door, or down the road a few miles, for most of my adult life. So she would flit in and bring a bite of this cake, often. She didn't bring more than a piece or two. Some of you know the why to this. She had a lifelong internal battle with her love for sweets, and her love for a 19-inch waistline. You read that correctly!!! 19 INCHES!!!

She is one of the few people I know that would eat mustard from a jar because she thought it counteracted the buttercream icing that she had just eaten from an old Cool Whip bowl in her fridge. Yes, Momma used Cool Whip bowls for Tupperware. Did your mom?

Every single day, she woke up early, and vowed to battle the FAT demons who chased her. And clearly, they never caught her. When she passed away at 88, in 2013, she still had a 19-inch waist I suppose. But my word, she loved a cake better than anyone I've ever known.

The difference between me and Momma? She walked her cake off. She walked five miles most days, up until she was 85 or 86.

Note to self. If you're going to bake these cakes?
Be like Momma. Eat a slice, and then take a walk!!!

CHRISTMAS CHOCOLATE MINT CAKE

INGREDIENTS

For the CAKE, you will need:
- 1 cup butter, softened
- 2 cups sugar
- 2 eggs
- 2 cups flour
- 2 teaspoons baking powder
- 1/2 teaspoon salt
- 1 cup cocoa
- 1 1/2 cups milk
- 2 cups mint chocolate morsels (Andes mints could be substituted.)
- 2 teaspoons vanilla

For the ICING, you will need:
- 1 1/2 cup mint chocolate morsels (Andes mints could be substituted.)
- 1 cup butter, softened
- 4 cups powdered sugar
- 2/3 cup cocoa powder
- 1/2 cup half and half
- 1/2 teaspoon peppermint extract (This is a strong flavor! Start with a drop or two and taste as you go. You can add more, but can't take it out.)

You MAY need:
- Peppermint candies, candy canes or other items to decorate the top of the cake, like we did! If you use Andes mints to replace the mint chips, you could always use those to decorate with, also. Either way this cake is a MINT sensation!

STEPS TO COOK

01. Preheat the oven to 350 degrees.
02. Beat butter at medium speed until creamy, add sugar and mix until fluffy. Add eggs, beat well. Combine flour, baking powder, salt and cocoa in a bowl. Add the half the dry ingredient mixture into creamed butter mix, combine well, add milk then remainder of the dry mixture. Scrape sides of bowl and mix until well blended. Stir in mint chocolate morsels and vanilla by hand. Pour batter into pans.

SUGGESTED PAN SIZE:
This cake recipe calls for two 9" round cake pans. Bake for 20-25 minutes.

TO MAKE THE ICING:
Melt the chocolate morsels in a microwave safe bowl in 30 second intervals, stirring after each time. Beat butter and melted morsels at medium speed until smooth and creamy. Add powdered sugar and cocoa, blend until well combined. Add half and half and peppermint extract, blend thoroughly.

Apply icing to the cake once it is cool. Top with candy canes or crushed candy pieces, as desired.

Cake can be stored in a container in the refrigerator for up to three days. This cake is typically gone before then!

This picture reminds me of Christmas. Christmas reminds me of Jesus, our redemption, the blessed hope of the Christ child. It also reminds me of family.

As most of you know, we are blessed. Our family is large, on purpose!! Ha!!

In 1991 my ex-husband and I created a blended family. And as I often say, the marriage lasted fifteen years, but the family will last forever. We chose love. I have written about this extensively in my other books, so sorry if it feels like a re-hash.

I'm going somewhere with this. After the divorce, when I met Steve, I tried to tell him. I am pretty sure he didn't "get" it! Steve and I married. He had lived the life of quiet bachelor for a few years. Quiet Christmases, quiet weekends, quiet everything it seems. Ha!! What had this man signed up for???

Christmas #1. I only had ten grandchildren at the time, six married kids, and six spouses. So the total, including Steve and I, was only 24 back in those days. Now, there's a total of 35. So it's a bit like a tribe on holidays!!

On this FIRST Christmas after I married Steve, I did my normal thing. I would shop for a day, and wrap for a day. Shop for a day, and wrap for a day. This was back before I started putting ALL of the presents for each child in their own large U-Haul box and wrapping them all together. This was when I did them all separately. So it was labor INTENSIVE! I hired a friend who was out of work to help me wrap. Krystal came and helped too. It was a bit like an assembly line. My motto is volume, I have LOTS of presents, even if they're inexpensive or just a "filler" type gift, I like for each child to have a lot to open. There's a reason for that. But we won't go into it here.

So on this Christmas, after assessing the assembly line wrapping, Steve looked scared. By Christmas, I could sense the nervousness in him. This is the man who bought gift cards, always. No wrapping, no "let's go big or go home" festive wife to drive him crazy.

The truth? My grandkids don't need a thing. I'm not trying to spoil them per se, I'm trying to create festivity!! Granny's house has provided a lifetime of Christmas memories. The games, the competitions, the traditions are part of what gives us roots. I'm always about fertilizing those roots!! It's never about money, it's about effort!!

Anyway, on Christmas Day, I had been up since dawn, cooking, finalizing the purse and wallet drawing for my adult kids. It's pretty overwhelming, actually. Steve looked scared to death. By the time the kids and grandkids arrived, he looked like someone who was observing the obliteration of the planet.

He was off to himself, staring at us from across the room. The kids tell this story and laugh!! He looked like a man who was in sheer shock!! When those grandkids starting tearing into those packages, all at once, I feared he may bolt out the garage door and never come back. He says that he was in awe. Overwhelmed. Lost for words. But I say He WAS thinking about running!!!

But he stayed. And yes. He's grown accustomed to the shenanigans of Christmas at Granny's house, and he's genteelly become the Poppa of this house!!

So, make the cake, and make it a party!! There's much to celebrate!!

MIKE'S BAHAMIAN RUM CAKE

INGREDIENTS

For the CAKE, you will need:
- 1/4 sugar, for coating the bundt pan
- 1 1/4 cups cake flour
- 1/4 teaspoon baking powder
- 1/2 teaspoon salt
- 1/8 teaspoon baking soda
- 3/4 cup + 1 tablespoon sugar, divided
- 5 tablespoons unsalted butter, melted and cooled
- 1/4 buttermilk, room temperature
- 1/4 dark or light rum, not spiced
- 1 1/2 tablespoon vegetable oil
- 1/2 tablespoon vanilla
- 3 egg yolks
- 1 large egg white

For the ICING, you will need:
- 1/4 cup butter
- 1/4 cup water
- 2 tablespoons pineapple juice
- 2 tablespoons dark or light rum, not spiced
- 1/2 cup white sugar

For the TOPPING:
- 1/4 cup sweetened coconut flakes

STEPS TO COOK

01.   Preheat the oven to 350 degrees.
02.   After you grease the pan apply the 1/4 cup of sugar to the inside of the pan. Gently tap and turn pan around until it is coated in sugar. In the bowl of a stand mixer stir together the flour, baking powder, salt, baking soda and 3/4 cup sugar. In a separate bowl whisk together the melted butter, buttermilk, rum, oil, vanilla and egg yolks until combined. In a third bowl, beat the egg white at medium-high speed until foamy, blend the remaining 1 tablespoon of sugar and beat until stiff peaks form. Set aside. Gradually pour the butter mixture into the flour mixture and mix on medium low speed until just combined. Remove from the stand mixer. Fold the whipped egg white into the cake batter until no streaks remain. Pour the batter evenly into the prepared pan.

SUGGESTED PAN SIZE:
This cake recipe calls for a well greased bundt cake pans. Bake for 30-35 minutes or until a toothpick comes out clean.

TO MAKE THE TOPPING:
While the cake is baking spread the coconut flakes on a baking sheet. Place them in the oven for about 5 minutes until toasted. Check them frequently.

TO MAKE THE SAUCE:
01.   Whisk together the sugar, butter and water in a saucepan. Bring to a boil over medium heat and boil or one minute. Mixture will be thick. Remove from the heat and carefully stir in the rum.

Once the cake has cooled slightly, poke holes all over the surface of the cake. Pour about half of the rum sauce over the cake, allowing it to sit for 5-10 minutes until it is absorbed. Carefully tip the cake onto a serving platter and drizzle the remaining sauce over the cake. Immediately sprinkle the toasted coconut over the cake, so it will adhere to the sauce.

This is the funniest story in this book!! At least I think it is.

In March of 2020, the Covid-19 pandemic struck, as you are well aware. I was in Florida. Some of the family ended up in Florida with us. We got several condos and told ourselves that the down time was needed. And then a week passed, two weeks passed, and the "what's going on here God?" thoughts took root.

Everyone was stressed. The cooking started. The diet flew out the window, for me at least. I had been on a healthy diet since January, but this pandemic stress was a real thing. Yes, I trusted God. But you know how it is. Cake was needed!!

Kelly, Mike, and girls were next door in a condo. Everyone was baking and cooking and praying!! One night Kelly said, "Mom. This may be the funniest thing I've ever had happen."

Kelly told me, "Hope called me in the bedroom. She said, 'Mom. I've known this for a couple of days. I didn't know if you could deal with it, but I have to tell you. I found RUM in Dad's computer bag!! Has he started drinking because he's stressed about this pandemic??'"

Bless it!! That baby thought her daddy had a problem!! It's a bit not funny, but so FUNNY to me!! So, no, Mike doesn't drink. He makes rum cakes!!!! And they are DIVINE!!!

HOT CHOCOLATE CAKE

INGREDIENTS

For the CAKE, you will need:
- 2 cups flour
- 2 cups sugar
- ¾ cup unsweetened cocoa powder
- 2 teaspoons baking soda
- 1 teaspoon salt
- 2 large eggs
- 1 cup milk
- 1 cup vegetable oil
- 1 1/2 teaspoons vanilla
- 1 cup hot water

For the ICING, you will need:
- 4 tablespoons hot water or milk
- 20 tablespoons hot chocolate powder mix
- 1 1/2 cup unsalted butter, room temperature
- 1 1/4 cup shortening
- 10 cups powdered sugar
- 2 teaspoons unsweetened cocoa powder
- 1-2 teaspoons water or milk

You MAY need:
- 1/2 cup unsalted butter, room temperature
- 1 cup powdered sugar
- 10 ounces marshmallow creme

Toppings: Large and/or small marshmallows

(Optional) For the GANACHE, you will need:
- 6 ounces white chocolate chips
- 3 tablespoons heavy whipping cream
- Mini marshmallows
- Marshmallow bits

STEPS TO COOK

01. Preheat the oven to 300 degrees.
02. Whisk together all dry ingredients in a mixing bowl, add in the eggs, milk, oil and vanilla. Mix until well blended. Add the hot water and mix until well combined. Place in prepared pans.

SUGGESTED PAN SIZE:
This cake recipe calls for two 8" round cake pans. Bake for 45-50 minutes. I would recommend lining the pans with parchment paper for this cake.

TO MAKE THE ICING:
01. Dissolve the hot chocolate powder into the water or milk, it will be thick! Set aside. In a mixing bowl, combine the butter and shortening until smooth and fluffy. Add about half of the powdered sugar and mix until well combined and smooth. Add the hot chocolate mixture and cocoa powder, mix until well combined. Add remaining powdered sugar and milk, as needed, until you get the desired consistency.

TO MAKE THE MARSHMALLOW FILLING:
Add the butter to a mixer bowl and beat until smooth. Add the powdered sugar and beat until well combined, scraping down the sides as needed. This may take a few minutes! Stir in the marshmallow cream and set filling aside.

(OPTIONAL) TO MAKE THE WHITE CHOCOLATE GANACHE:
Add the white chocolate chips to a medium sized bowl, heat the cream just until it begins to boil, then pour it over the chocolate. Whisk the mixture together so it begins to melt. Heat for an additional 10 seconds, whisking vigorously. Heat again, if needed.

Instructions for assembling the cake: When cake is cooled, use a serrated knife to divide each cake into two layers, creating 4 layers total. Place the first layer on a cake plate and apply about half a cup of hot chocolate frosting, spreading it evenly over the layer. Pipe an edge or dam around the edge of the cake and fill it with 3/4 cup of marshmallow filling. Spread into an even layer. Repeat until you get to the top layer. On the top layer, spread a crumb coat of icing on top and sides of cake, refrigerate for about an hour to allow filling to firm up. (This keeps the layers from slipping when applying the icing.) Remove from refrigerator, frost the outside of the cake. Pile up marshmallows on top for the presentation seen here!

If you made the chocolate ganache, using a spoon or a squeeze bottle, drizzle ganache around the edge of the cake, running from under the marshmallows and down the sides of the cake.

If making cake ahead of time, refrigerate cake until ready to serve. When serving, remove from refrigerator 1-2 hours in advance to come up to temperature. Cake can be stored in a container in the refrigerator for up to three days. This cake is typically gone before then!

My family loves hot chocolate. I like it, but these kids ABSOLUTELY LOVE it!!

These girls were born within a year's time. Hannah in September, Ashleigh in February, and then Katelanne in September. To know them, is to love them!!

I took them to New York last year for Hannah and Ashleigh's 16th birthday. That was before the craziness of the pandemic and these awful riots! We went to a Broadway show, and afterwards they talked me into taking them to a sugar shack called The Sugar Factory. Look, I'm gullible when it comes to these kids. They said, "We will share!!" They ordered a big fizzy drink, and I'm thinking one dessert, and it was like 79 dollars, or something like that!! Holy cow!! That's some expensive sugar.

But I promise, this cake will hit the spot, it's their favorite, and it won't cost you an airfare to New York City or 79 dollars! Ha!!

These girls are my heart!! And aren't they beautiful?

GERMAN CHOCOLATE CAKE

INGREDIENTS

For the CAKE, you will need:
- 1 package baker's German sweet chocolate (4 ounces)
- 1/2 cup boiling water
- 1 cup butter or margarine
- 2 cups sugar
- 4 eggs, separated
- 1 teaspoon vanilla
- 2 cups all purpose flour
- 1 teaspoon baking soda
- 1/2 teaspoon salt
- 1 cup buttermilk
- 1/2 to 1 teaspoon instant espresso powder (optional but recommended)

For the ICING, you will need:
- 1 1/2 cup sugar
- 1 1/2 cups evaporated milk
- 4 large egg yolks, room temperature and lightly beaten
- 3/4 cup unsalted butter or margarine
- 1 1/2 teaspoon vanilla
- 2 cups sweetened shredded coconut
- 1 1/2 cup chopped pecans

STEPS TO COOK

01. Preheat the oven to 350 degrees.
02. Melt chocolate in boiling water, allow to cool.
03. Beat egg whites until stiff peaks form, set aside.
04. Combine flour, soda and salt and set aside.
05. In a mixing bowl, cream together butter and sugar until light and fluffy. Beat in egg yolks and scrape down the sides of the bowl. Stir in vanilla extract and cooled chocolate. Beat in the flour mixture alternately with the buttermilk, beginning and ending with the dry mixture. Fold egg whites into mixture. Pour into pans.

SUGGESTED PAN SIZE:

This cake recipe calls for three 9" round cake pans. Bake for 25-30 minutes.

TO MAKE THE ICING:
First: In a saucepan combine evaporated milk, sugar, beaten egg yolks, butter and vanilla. Cook and stir over medium heat until thickened and then remove from heat. Stir in shredded coconut and pecans. Allow to cool until thick enough to spread.

Apply icing to the cake once it is cool.

Cake can be stored in a container in the refrigerator for up to three days.
This cake is typically gone before then!

This is the first FROM SCRATCH cake I ever made. I was about eighteen or nineteen years old, and one day I decided I would master this cake thing. Now remember, I was a young bride, I couldn't cook, and I had lots of random obstacles in this season of life. Honestly, I have experienced obstacles in ALL seasons, as have you, I'm confident. But hey, God is always good, and so is cake!! That's what we're doing here, reminding you of that!!

Anyway, I marched myself into Bob's IGA Foodliner in Hartford, Kentucky. Remember, my cake baking experience was limited to a box cake and an icing mix. I don't think we had pre-made icing back in the early seventies. This has been a very long time ago, and I can't pretend to tell you that I remember a lot about this experience. But what I do remember is this. I felt like I had to have SO MANY ingredients. Who knew?? I had no clue that cake making called for all of this.

And holy cow. Buttermilk in a cake?? Game changer. And I learned this too. Those egg yolks, sugar, and evaporated milk, when combined and cooked?? Best thing I had ever tasted!!!

Back to the buttermilk. I don't drink buttermilk. I was SO grossed out that this cake was going to contain buttermilk. But oh my, when I tasted the batter, yes I'm that girl. This batter, I could have guzzled it. The smell of the chocolate, that thing that buttermilk brings to the party, I shall never forget it.

How sad is it that I can remember cake experiences from a half a century ago, yet I struggle to remember how much my kids weighed at birth!! Ha!!

This cake is better the second day, if it's covered. If you've never made a German Chocolate cake? It should be on your bucket list. If for no other reason than to lick the bowl!!

My granddaughters have a variation that's iced in pre-made chocolate icing on the sides!! That's what's pictured.

Also, I often ice ONLY the top and the layers, no sides!! Ice it any way you please, make it your own!!! Just don't leave out the buttermilk!!!

KENTUCKY'S BEST JAM CAKE

This cake is a tradition in Kentucky! While the ingredient list is lengthy, it is well worth the shopping list. Follow the straight-forward steps and you will have a cake that will take you back to every grandmother's house in Kentucky!

INGREDIENTS

For the CAKE, you will need:
- 5 eggs separated
- 1 teaspoon cinnamon
- 2 teaspoons of cloves
- 1 teaspoon nutmeg
- 2 teaspoons of baking soda
- 1 cup buttermilk
- 2 cups of sugar
- 1/2 cup of Crisco shortening
- 1 cup of pecans
- 1 cup of raisins
- 1 cup of strawberry preserves
- 2 cups of blackberry preserves
- 1 cup pineapple, apricot or peach preserves

For the ICING, you will need:
- 1 cup evaporated milk
- 1 cup sugar
- 3 egg yolks
- 1/4 pound of margarine or butter
- 1 teaspoon vanilla
- 1 1/3 angel flake coconut
- 1 cup chopped pecans

STEPS TO COOK

For this particular cake recipe, I recommend doubling the icing recipe!

01. Preheat the oven to 350 degrees.
02. Dissolve baking soda in buttermilk.
02. Separate the egg yolks from the egg whites. Beat egg whites until stiff until set aside.
04. Cream butter, sugar and Crisco until blended well, then add egg yolks.
05. Sift together flour, cinnamon, cloves and baking soda then add the buttermilk to this dry mixture.
06. Add the mix of dry ingredients and buttermilk to the creamed mixture. Mix well.
07. Stir in pecans, raisins and all preserves.
08. Fold in egg whites.

Blend until smooth, but don't over mix the batter. Pour into pans.

<u>**SUGGESTED PAN SIZE**</u>:
This cake recipe calls for six 9" round cake pans. You heard it right, six pans!
Bake for 20 minutes.

<u>**TO MAKE THE ICING**</u>:
Combine evaporated milk, sugar, egg yolks, margarine or butter and vanilla, stir over medium heat until thick approximately 12 minutes. Stir in coconut and pecans.
Beat until thick enough to spread.

Layers should be assembled into two 3-tier cakes with icing between layers and icing all over. I recommend doubling the icing recipe.

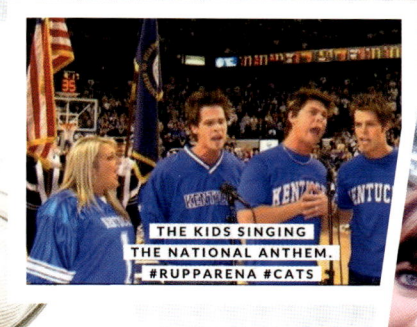

Photo captions:
- THE KIDS SINGING THE NATIONAL ANTHEM. #RUPPARENA #CATS
- The house on Navaho Dr, 55 years after the chicken incident

My momma's family always made jam cakes. Back in Kentucky, where I come from, folks make blackberry preserves, JUST so they can make jam cakes. My Aunt Net and my momma made them every year for Christmas and Thanksgiving. They wouldn't dream of having a Christmas without jam cake.

So, once again: When I'm fortunate enough to have a slice, it's a taste of home. Sometimes, I feel sorry for those of you who have never eaten a tomato while picking them from the garden...or licked the wooden spoon of the dark purple blackberry syrup that was being gingerly poured into Mason jars on a hot August afternoon.

Now, don't let me mislead you. I didn't grow up on a farm. I lived in a subdivision as a child, just like I do as an adult. But Momma and Daddy had left the farm so that Dad could start a lucrative business. I was two when the Beverly Hillbillies loaded up the truck and moved to town!! Ha!

However, my siblings are considerably older, and they talked about the "days before Kathy was born" as if it was a dispensation of time. Ha-Ha!! They had it tough, they walked to school, and they didn't have a big house with multiple bathrooms.

They had a path and an outdoor toilet. Truth, they did.

But Momma brought enough "country" to our house on Navaho Drive to introduce me to the art of canning. You couldn't take the country out of her!!

Once, when I was a little girl, I came home from school...to our suburban neighborhood. Our neighbor on the left was a Jewish jeweler, the neighbor on the right was an attorney, the neighbor behind us? A physician. You get my drift. They weren't killing pigs in their yard or anything. This was before the HOA rules that followed in the subsequent decades. But, my momma may have been the reason that an HOA was necessary.

Yep, You guessed it. I came home from school to what looked like a massacre!!!! She had bought a truckload of chickens!!! And she was ringing their necks, and preparing them for the freezer...IN OUR DRIVEWAY!!!! Not even kidding.

My momma was one-of-a-kind, and I miss her every single day!!

Back to the cake: My friend Ruth, got this recipe from her sweet mother-in-law many years ago!! And I must tell you!! It's THE BEST JAM cake recipe you will ever find!!! Make it, and be prepared to be impressed!!! You will love this little taste of my old KENTUCKY home!!

ANNETA'S CARROT CAKE

INGREDIENTS

For the CAKE, you will need:
- 2 cup flour
- 1 1/2 teaspoon baking soda
- 1 teaspoon salt
- 2 teaspoons cinnamon
- 1 1/2 cups vegetable or canola oil
- 2 cups sugar
- 4 eggs
- 1 teaspoon vanilla
- 2 cups grated carrots
- 1 can crushed pineapple (15 ounces)
- 1 3/4 cups chopped nuts
- 1 cup raisins
- 1 cup dates
- 1 cup coconut

For the FILLING, you will need:
- 1 cup evaporated milk
- 1 cup sugar
- 3 egg yolks
- 1 teaspoon vanilla
- 1/2 cup margarine or butter
- 1 cup chopped nuts
- 1 cup coconut

For the ICING, you will need:
- 1 pack of cream cheese (8 ounces), softened
- 1 stick butter or margarine, softened
- 1 box of powdered sugar
- 2 teaspoons vanilla

STEPS TO COOK

01. Preheat the oven to 325 degrees.
02. Sift together flour, baking soda, salt, cinnamon and set aside. Mix oil, sugar, eggs and vanilla until combined. Add dry ingredient mixture and mix well. Add carrots, nuts, pineapple, raisins, dates and coconut. Blend until smooth, but don't over mix the batter. Pour into pans.

SUGGESTED PAN SIZE:
This cake recipe calls for four 9" round cake pans. Bake for 30-35 minutes. You can also use two 9" x 13" pans.

TO MAKE THE FILLING:
In a saucepan, combine milk, sugar, butter, egg yolks and vanilla cook until thickened over medium heat. Add chopped nuts and coconut, beat until well combined. Spread between layers of cake.

This mixture can also be applied to the top layer of the cake if desired, either under the icing or instead of the icing.

TO MAKE THE ICING:
01. In a bowl, mix cream cheese and butter and beat until combined. Gradually add powdered sugar and vanilla.

Apply icing to the cake once it is cool.

Personal note from Kathy: *I do three layers, thicker layers, and I add a bit of icing in the middle, after the filling drizzles in.*

My girls associate carrot cake with my sister Anneta. Apparently, some of their earliest cake comas were induced by Anneta's famous carrot cake!! I don't remember the first time I had it, and I don't remember the last time, but I remember many times in between. This cake is a perfect example of the memory making that food promotes.

When I mentioned doing this cakebook, Krystal and Kelly both, at different times, said, "Oh Mom, Anneta's carrot cake!!! You must include it."

That cake invokes emotions in them, memories of a simpler time. Our childhood memories are always back there, waiting for the smell of cinnamon to induce them to come forward and crowd out the business of the day. When I smell cinnamon, I can close my eyes and be back in Beaver Dam!!

It takes me back to a younger me, a healthy Anneta, a vibrant Momma, a big extended family....all vying for the first piece of cake, while it's still warm.

Anneta isn't as healthy as she once was, Momma is gone, and the extended family is scattered all over the country. Time marches on. No one can stop father time. He's a hateful cuss!!

But today, as I type and allow my memories to own this day, I'm thankful for the effort. I'm thankful that Anneta took the time to grate those carrots. She could have bought a cake mix. I'm thankful for her southern hospitality. She was the most gracious hostess in town, back in the day. Truly, her example molded my hospitality goals. If she had food, the world had food. If they needed to grill a dozen burgers for their family and friends, they would throw on another dozen in case neighbors dropped in.

I always cook WAY more than I need. And most people think it's because I have ALL of these kids and grandkids. But the truth is this. It started many years before. It's how she taught me by example. I'm thankful. I don't regret one minute of labor or one dollar spent. As I often say, it's my love language. If I can feed you, I've loved you.

Take some time and make this cake. Allow yourself to enjoy the aroma!! I don't do candles because of allergies, and I so ENJOY baking these wonderful smelling cakes, and allowing the NATURAL smells to make me happy!!!

PERFECT POUND CAKE

INGREDIENTS

For the CAKE, you will need:
- 3 cups sugar
- 3 cups sifted cake flour
- 2 sticks salted butter, room temperature
- 6 eggs, room temperature
- 1 block cream cheese, room temperature
- 1 teaspoon vanilla

STEPS TO COOK

01. Do NOT preheat oven
02. Cream butter, cream cheese and sugar until light and fluffy. Mix in eggs one at a time, mixing for one minute after adding each egg. Gradually add in the flour and vanilla extract. Blend until smooth, but don't over mix the batter. Pour into pan.

SUGGESTED PAN SIZE:
This cake recipe calls for a well greased and floured bundt cake pans. Place cake into a COLD oven and turn the oven on to 300 degrees. Bake for 80-90 minutes. Check cake with a toothpick.

This pound cake should yield you a delicious, crunchy top! And it is the BOMB when served with no topping, actually, one of my favorite foods.

However, it's the kind of cake you can make, freeze, and grab when you need to randomly entertain. When the family is driving in from out of town for the day, and they don't give you a heads up!!

To top this heavenly cake: Strawberries are wonderful, fresh peaches, a spoonful of blackberry preserves, or just fresh whipped cream!!

To make a delicious whipped cream to serve, simply put a cup of whipping cream in a bowl, whip until it forms a peak, add a teaspoon of vanilla, and a tablespoon of powdered sugar, or table sugar. Either will work!! It's scrumptious!!

Happily, pound cake is exceptionally easy to bake and nearly impossible to mess up!! Since a GOOD pound cake needs to be neither airy nor delicate, it's hard to mess up the batter. Named for the traditional proportions of ingredients - a pound of butter + a pound of flour + a pound of sugar + a pound of eggs - modern pound cakes riff a bit on the historical formula.

This cake is very good plain. Dangerously good, I might say. For instance, if you were to offer me a slice that you had stashed in your freezer and hadn't wrapped properly, I would eat it. Freezer burn and all. And I'd eat it while talking and get crumbs all over your floor!! And by the way, the best way to wrap a pound cake for freezing, is Saran wrap. Then I won't get the freezer burn piece when I come over!! Ha!!

The love for me and pound cake rests in one ingredient. BUTTER!! The other ingredients are the background singers, the butter is the lead vocalist!! Most cakes have the sweet butter blended in, but squarely behind the bolder flavorings of chocolate, strawberry, lemon, etc.

But this cake allows me to taste, in EVERY SINGLE BITE, my favorite taste experience. Sweet, creamy, salted butter!!!

When Kelly was little, she too loved butter!! The apple doesn't fall far from the tree!!

When she was about 18 months-old, we lived with my in-laws while we were building a house. My mother-in-law was a fabulous cook. Her biscuits were homemade, buttermilk biscuits. She would no more serve a canned biscuit than she would serve a frozen chicken pot-pie. Her food standards were HIGH!!

Anyway, Kelly was less than two years old, and already Mamaw Betty had created a LOVE for butter and biscuits in this child. Mamaw Betty would butter a biscuit for her, but the butter melted immediately on the warm biscuit. Kelly would cry and say, "My butter is gone, I need more butter!" Mamaw would butter it again, and depending on the temperature of this biscuit, maybe a third time. All the while that butter was soaking that biscuit.

That baby needed to SEE that butter to believe it was there! Well sometimes butter is a bit like faith. We can't see it, but we just know it's there!!!

When you eat this cake, you can TASTE that sweet butter. I encourage you to make two of these. Eat one, and freeze the other!!! I don't FREEZE DESSERTS!! But this is the exception to the freezing rule.

CLASSIC YELLOW CAKE WITH CHOCOLATE FROSTING

This cake recipe is a classic go-to cake. Combine it with chocolate frosting or whatever flavor combination is your favorite! It can easily be dressed up with crushed candies in between the layers and on top, candy bars, sprinkles or any other treats. Get creative and make it uniquely yours!

INGREDIENTS

For the CAKE, you will need:
- 3 sticks butter, room temperature
- 2 cups sugar
- 3 eggs, room temperature
- 3 egg yolks, room temperature
- 1 teaspoon vanilla extract
- 3 cups cake flour
- 1 teaspoon baking powder
- 1/2 teaspoon baking soda
- 1/2 teaspoon salt
- 1 cup nonfat buttermilk

For the ICING, you will need:
- 12 ounces semi-sweet chocolate, finely chopped
- 1 cup heavy cream
- 1 cup butter, room temperature
- 1 cup powdered sugar
- 1/4 teaspoon kosher salt
- 1/2 teaspoon vanilla extract

You MAY need:
- Sprinkles, Candies, Candy Pieces, Candy Bars or other toppings

STEPS TO COOK

01. Preheat the oven to 350 degrees.
02. Cream together butter and sugar until light and fluffy. This may take a few minutes. Scrape down the sides and bottom of the bowl during this process. In a small bowl whisk together eggs, egg yolks and vanilla just until combined. Set aside. Slow mixer to low and gently add egg mixture to creamed ingredients, mix just until combined. Increase speed and blend for 30 seconds. In a bowl, sift together flour, salt, baking powder and baking soda. On low speed, mix in alternately the flour mixture and buttermilk, just scrape down sides and bottom of the mixing bowl. Blend by hand until smooth, but don't over mix the batter. Pour into pans.

<u>**SUGGESTED PAN SIZE**</u>:

This cake recipe calls for two 8" round cake pans. Bake for 40-50 minutes or until golden brown.

<u>**TO MAKE THE ICING**</u>:

01. Place the chopped chocolate in a heat-proof bowl. In a small saucepan, scald the cream over medium-high heat (bubbles start to form around the edge of the pan, but the cream is not boiling). Pour the hot cream over the chocolate and let sit for about 1 minute, then slowly whisk together the chocolate and cream until the chocolate is completely melted and the mixture is smooth. Let sit at room temperature for 1-2 hours, or until completely cool. (Or, refrigerate the ganache until cool, about 30 minutes, whisking every 10 minutes).
02. In a mixing bowl, beat the butter on medium-low speed until smooth. Add the powdered sugar, salt, and vanilla and continue to beat on medium-low speed until the mixture is fluffy and smooth. Scrape down the bowl and the paddle. Add the cooled ganache and mix until completely combined. Scrape the sides and bottom of the bowl. Mix on medium-high for about 1 minute, or until the frosting lightens in color and thickens. (Use the frosting the day you make it, or cover and store in the refrigerator for up to 1 day, then bring to room temperature and paddle again for a few minutes until smooth before using.)

Apply icing to the cake once it is cool. Add any toppings desired.

When I look at this picture, I am reminded of a story!! About twenty-five years ago I went through a phase of pranksterism. That's probably not a word. But I am sure you get it. I love a joke, a hang!!

One day I was at a craft store and noticed that the shape of the green foam that you place flowers in to make an arrangement for a table, graveside, or what have you...was the exact same size as a layer of cake. Bingo. I bought a dozen or more. Then I hurriedly trucked my little mischievous self back to Beaver Dam. I was living in Kentucky, and was in Owensboro shopping. That was back when I shopped!!! Ha!! Before Amazon and pandemics.

I took my foam CAKES in the kitchen, whipped up some chocolate icing, layered those foam cakes three tiers high. I piled the icing on, garnished with candy, and put that thing in the prettiest cake stand I owned. I drove the three miles to Mom and Noble's house. My step-dad was a character, in a good way. He WAS FUNNY!!! The first time he met Steve, we had only had a couple of dates, he said, "Boy, you built a front porch bigger than your shed!"

I was like, "Did you just say his stomach was big with your clever analogy?" Ha!! That was Noble.

But on this day, I had him!! I walked in and said, "Noble, I've made you a cake! JUST for you." He loved a chocolate iced cake. I said, "Momma, don't you cut this. It's his. Let him cut the first piece."

He took a knife and started to cut, I could hear him muttering under his breath, "She didn't unthaw it." This went on for several minutes. Finally, he said, "Kat, you need to stick to playing the piano and leave the cake making to your momma!!"

FRIDAY NIGHT CUPCAKES

INGREDIENTS

For the CUPCAKE, you will need:
- 1 1/8 cups flour ; all purpose
- 1 1/2 tsp. baking powder
- 1/2 tsp. salt
- 1/3 cup butter ; softened
- 1/2 cup brown sugar
- 1/4 cup white sugar
- 1 large egg
- 1/2 cup milk
- 1/2 tsp. pure vanilla extract
- 8 Hershey's chocolate kisses ; unwrapped

STEPS TO COOK

01. Preheat oven to 350 degrees..
02. Line muffin tin with cupcake papers. You will need about 8 or 9...fill the empty ones half way with water so that the pan doesn't burn.
03. Whisk together the flour, baking powder and salt. Set aside.
04. In a large bowl, cream both sugars with the butter. Then beat in the egg and vanilla extract. Then beat in the flour mixture, alternating with the milk. Mix til just incorporated.
05. Fill muffin cups 1/3 full. Then place a chocolate kiss in the center. Top with more batter til 2/3 full.
06. Bake on center rack for 18 - 20 minutes or until center of cupcake springs back when lightly touched.

Remove from oven and let cool completely before frosting.

This only makes 8 to 10 cupcakes!! If you're me? You're doubling or tripling!!

Ice with your favorite icing. And enjoy!!

In 1994, as I often discuss, we left the NORMAL of home, for the most part. The following decade was spent on a bus. In 1995 we spent over 300 days on the road. 1996 was worse.

We had left the normalcy of the known, to seek a musical road that was unknown, scary at best, and truly... in retrospect, a bit stupid. For I was an adult, making big girl decisions that involved all of these kids, and their collective future. The boys liked to play basketball, but you can't play basketball when you're in Timbuktu loading a bus.

The girls weren't "sporty" per se, but they also forfeited normal football game weekends, and hometown boyfriends. Notice they married out-of-town guys, that they met on the road.

Terah went on the road when she was about 13 or 14. I have no regrets, thanks to Jesus and the hard work of these kids...all is well. I told God that if He would give us bread and water, we would never look back. No turning around. God has more than supplied. We got cake too!! Ha!!

All kidding aside, these kids sacrificed greatly. But what a blessed life they live. And about now I want to point out this little bit of info. Not everyone is called to sing, preach, play an instrument, be a Bible scholar. They're just not!!

Krystal my oldest doesn't sing. Yet, she's gifted in a million other ways. Her voice is heard, her skill set is used, always. She can do anything, literally. I've watched the non-singing grandchildren. I've watched the singing grandchildren. The Bowling girls have grown up on a bus. Logan, Terah's 16 year-old, has grown up in public school. He's well rounded, smart and extremely gifted at sports, football specifically.

The Bowling girls are smart as whips, completely socially adjusted, and yet...they have missed more school than they attended, due to the road schedule. So there's no judgment from me either way. The parents have to figure it out. And they have.

I realized I didn't have this awesome cupcake recipe in this book!! And I realized that this football playing man-child loves a cupcake, and he LOVES some Friday Night LIGHTS!!! So this is for you, Logan!

Make these little jewels, they are delish!! And say an extra prayer tonight, and always, for my little high school football player, Logan, who is more than a foot taller than me!! Pray safety and favor over him!! He's a sweet boy who loves Jesus, and is unashamed!!

God can use his talent on a world stage!! And this one will always be my little boy, no matter how tall he gets!

STEVE'S HOT PEPPER CORN CAKE

INGREDIENTS

You will need:
- 2 ¼ cups self rising yellow corn meal mix
- 3 eggs
- 1 cup shredded cheddar cheese
- 15 ounce can of cream corn
- 1 stick of melted butter
- 1 cup buttermilk
- ¾ cup sour cream
- 15 to 20 jalapeno pepper rings. I use the ones in a jar, not fresh.
- Two chili peppers, diced.

STEPS TO COOK

01. Preheat oven to 350.

You truly need a large iron skillet, but if you don't have one, use the largest skillet that you have that is oven safe, or an extra large casserole dish as a last resort.

02. Oil your pan and heat by placing in a hot oven. Any vegetable oil or olive oil is fine. Do not use butter for this.

03. Mix your ingredients by hand in a large bowl. Pour in the hot pan and bake for 45 to 55 minutes, or until done!! Garnish with chilis or jalapenos, if you dare!!

This is great with soups, chili, a southern meat and three dinner, or by itself with a slab of creamy butter!!! Holy cow!!

The truth about this recipe? I would rather have this for dinner than anything I can think of!!

When we decided to include some non-sweet cakes, this was my first choice!!

Make it, eat it, repent later!!!

Most of you know a bit about my husband, Steve. If you've read my books, you know him. I describe him to a T. When Steve laughs the world becomes a better place. The earth shakes a little. This man laughs like no one else in the world. The kids call his laugh "the jack-hammer." He makes an up-and-down motion with his entire body. It starts on the inside and works it's way out. Once it's a full body laugh, EVERYONE is laughing. It's infectious.

Our first date was to a Mexican restaurant. It was not at all a swanky place. The tables were sticky, the glasses were those tall, red plastic restaurant glasses, and it was clear to me that he wasn't trying to impress. And if you know me, you know that was the best thing he could have done. I despise pretention!!!

If I had never seen him again, if there had been no second date, I would remember one thing about the realtor from Hendersonville, Steve. He liked salsa. He liked hot food too!! We sat at the unimpressive restaurant for hours. We talked about everything, and nothing. He thought my kids had a garage band and probably didn't have jobs. He asked me if they had aspirations to make a living in music. I laughed and loved him for it. He had no clue that music had been our livelihood for more than a decade.

That's why there was a second date. He didn't care about my life. He seemed to care about me. He wasn't concerned about what I could give him or not, he was concerned about my thoughts on politics, morals, and jalapenos!! Ha!!

The rest is sort of history I suppose. We've had a gazillion meals together in the fourteen years of bliss. And yes, there's a common denominator to almost EVERY single meal. Steve gets out a huge container of black pepper and covers his food before the eating frenzy begins. If you know him, you're shaking your head right now!! You know I'm telling the truth. Ha!!

And about two bites in he gets up and grabs a jar of jalapeno peppers!! NO MATTER what we're having. Soup? Yes. Spaghetti? Yes. Chicken? Yes. Salad? Yes.

He cares not what you and I think of him. He's eating the peppers!! He eats them and sweats!! I ask him, "Why would you do that? Isn't that a bit miserable??"

His response is always the same, "I love it."

I don't understand it, I never will!! But that's okay. Steve is an original!! And I am rarely with him on the peppers, but Lord have mercy y'all, when cornbread is involved?

I am 100% in!!! Make it and you will see!!

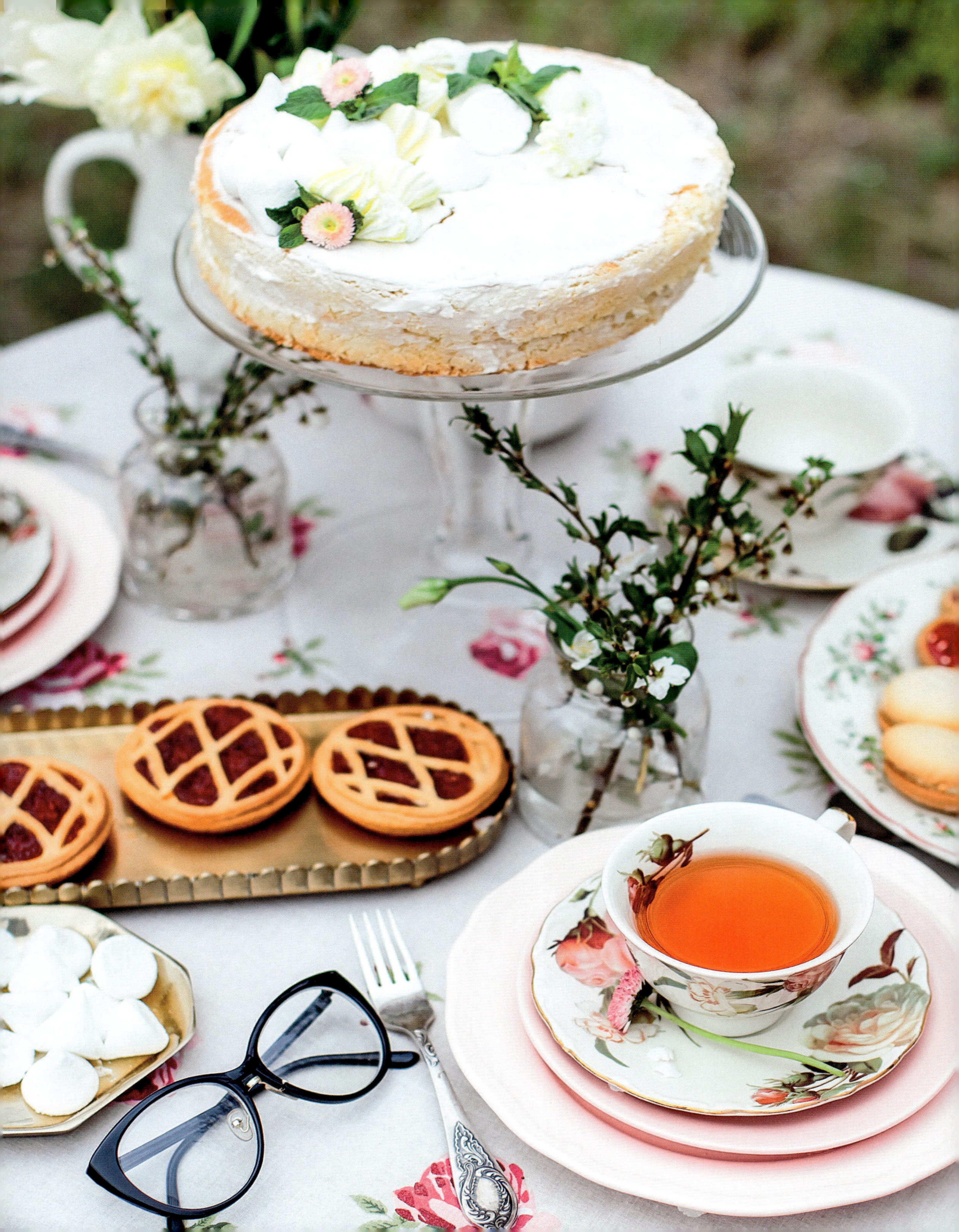

Spring

If we had never experienced a cold treacherous winter, the beautiful blossoms of spring would not be nearly as appreciated. If we had never been hungry, we wouldn't appreciate the labor and satisfaction of a luscious homemade cake. If we had never felt hopeless, we wouldn't understand the peace that only Jesus brings. Seasons. Let's celebrate each of them.

I will never tire of seeing the first daffodil, or as Momma called them…the Easter flowers. Something inside me stirs, every single year. For that little yellow flower reminds me that nature is renewable. The cold harsh winter was tough, but those strong roots are down there, buried beneath the frozen ground. Waiting. For there's another year, another Easter, another reason to bloom.

The great gift of Easter is hope. You're redeemable. I'm redeemable. The most awful person, the one on the news last night, he's redeemable. What a plot twist that was to the religious folk in Jesus's day.

And yes, it's still a complex way of thinking. You can't buy it, earn it, become GOOD enough or smart enough.

Salvation, the ultimate fix for the likes of us, was established one Friday, about two thousand years ago.

Springtime. The tomb is empty. And there's a million and one reasons to celebrate.

If you're a Christ follower, this season should be as sweet as honey to you. For you are in the big party plan. The redeemed of the Lord, we're all invited.

And what a menu we shall have. But until then? We will make a coconut cake and bake a ham. Loving the lives we have, but longing for HIS appearing!!!

What a blessed people we are!!!

And yes!!! Let the redeemed of the LORD say so.

BEST FRIEND COCONUT CAKE

INGREDIENTS

For the CAKE, you will need:
- 1 cup of water
- 1/3 cup of butter, softened
- 3 eggs
- Box of your favorite yellow cake mix

For the ICING, you will need:
- 1 bag of sweetened shredded coconut
- 1 small container of sour cream (8 ounces)
- 2 cups of sugar
- 1 large container of Cool Whip

STEPS TO COOK

01. Preheat the oven to 350 degrees.
02. Beat cake mix, eggs, water and softened butter. Blend until smooth, but don't over mix the batter. Pour into pans.

SUGGESTED PAN SIZE:
This cake recipe calls for two 9" round cake pans. Bake for 25-30 minutes.

TO MAKE THE ICING:
01. In a bowl, combine sour cream, sugar, thawed Cool Whip and 1/3 of the bag of coconut. Spread between layers and ice cake thoroughly with mixture.
02. Spread remaining coconut on the top and sides of the cake.

Apply icing to the cake once it is cool.

Cake can be stored in a container in the refrigerator for up to three days. This cake is typically gone before then!

Linda and I have been eating cake together for over fifty years. We've seen a lot of good cakes in our lifetime! We've had birthday cakes, baby shower cakes (a hundred years ago when we were having babies) and my favorite?? The "just because" cakes.

Linda has been my friend through every season of life. We've had a few "just because" moments. She's the friend that was patiently sitting in the waiting room with Steve and the kids while they stopped my heart, and proceeded with the LONG, SCARY open-heart surgery. She's the friend that wiped those divorce tears, took those 2 am phone calls, and helped patch me back together when no one thought it could be done.

The world thought I was too broken for a comeback. But Linda didn't. She has a way of suggesting and encouraging those around her.

The test of a GREAT recipe is a bit like the test of a GREAT friendship. Some friends are here for the party. Here for the fun times, but no-where to be found when you're in year two of YOUR season of grief. They could hang for six months or so, but my goodness. They're tired, and they're out.

They're the cake with shimmery sprinkles, but dry as a bone. Someone forgot to add the butter or the oil. It's like sawdust inside. The cute little sprinkles are nice, but the substance is in the batter, and it ain't happening.

I've made a few of those cakes. And, I've had a LOT of those friends. Pretty sprinkles on the outside, fluffy pink icing, but dry enough to choke a camel.

And then there's the Linda's of the world. They are few. And they are far between. Your momma was right. To have a friend that loves ALWAYS is a gift that gold cannot buy.

Girls like Linda are the coconut cakes of the world. Fluffy, tried, and true.

I am blessed with several "Lindas" in my life. But make no mistake, she is the original! She makes this cake, and she actually provided me with this photo!! It's as good as it looks!!

Make it, and call YOUR coconut cake friends over to share. This cake is divine!!

And I can't believe I just called my friend a coconut cake. Me and my analogies!!

THE CRABB-TURTLE CHEESECAKE

INGREDIENTS

For the CAKE, you will need:
- 2 cups Oreo Chocolate Cookie Crumbs
- 2 Tbsp butter or margarine, melted
- 1 bag (14 oz.) KRAFT Caramels
- 1/2 cup milk
- 3 pkg (8 oz. each) PHILADELPHIA Cream Cheese, softened
- 3/4 cup sugar
- 1 Tbsp vanilla
- 3 eggs
- 1/2 cup Planters Pecan pieces
- 2 squares Baker's Semi-Sweet Baking Chocolate

STEPS TO COOK

01. Mix crumbs and butter; press onto bottom and 2 inches up side of 9-inch springform pan.

02. Place caramels and milk in small microwave bowl. Microwave on High 3 minutes or until caramels are completely melted, stirring after each minute. Pour 1/2 of the caramel mixture into crust. Refrigerate 10 minutes. Set remaining caramel mixture aside for later use.

03. Beat cream cheese, sugar, and vanilla with electric mixer on medium until well blended. Add eggs, 1 at a time, mixing on low after each addition until blended. Pour over caramel mixture in crust.

04. If using a silver springform pan, bake at 325°F for 1 hour 5 minutes to 1 hour 10 minutes or until center is almost set. If using a dark non-stick springform pan, bake at 300°F for 1 hour 5 minutes or 1 hour 10 minutes or until center is almost set. Run knife or metal spatula around side of pan to loosen cake; cool before removing side of pan.

05. Refrigerate 4 hours or overnight. Top with remaining caramel mixture and pecans just before serving. Melt chocolate on low in a sauce pan, drizzle over cheesecake.

So you looked at the name and laughed. Right??

Eli and Ean, Aaron and Amanda's sons, love a sweet. Ean, my little ice cream eating buddy...had rather have a dessert than a box full of money. He's my grandchild!!

As I sit here and ponder, trying to pair people with desserts, pictures with memories...I am taking many trips down memory lane. It's actually been a fun little week of traveling, and I haven't left my office.

I was trying to think of a clever name that would please Eli, as this is his appointed dessert. Ha!! He's a comic of sorts, a bit of sarcasm mixed with the mannerism of a class clown. So, I think he will be proud of the confusing, yet appropriate name.

I can just hear Myrtle in Omaha, "Oh my gosh Howard, this crazy book has a seafood cheesecake in it!!!!" Uhm, no Myrtle. It's a little play on words!! Ha!!

Reminds me of a story. Steve says that going to the bathroom reminds me of a story. Ha!! I am not sure Steve is wrong. But back to my story.

Kentucky, 1994. The musical dreams of the family were being birthed, shaped...if you will. I write about this extensively in my book, Stronger. But I must expound, if only for a moment.

The music?? I knew that God was in it. Many people recognized that "something" that was on them. I often say that Nashville is full of singers that you will never hear of. They can out-sing the best singers in town, or out-play the best musicians in town. And yet, they're waiting tables and working at hotels. The difference between success and failure can be a variety of things.

Hard work is a must. Also, unity!! The unity was clear. It was one for all, all for one. They didn't even realize how unselfish they were. That unity has kept them, even now....it's one of the elements that changes the atmosphere when they step on stage. And of course, the anointing that falls on those who allow it, that's the big one. It's something they have ALWAYS understood.

When I realized that the kids had a future...I enlisted some professional opinions. I invited a dozen or more movers and shakers, from Nashville, to come hear them in Kentucky. Of course, I had to entice them with a free weekend in a resort, show tickets, and lots of crab legs!! Not Crabb legs, but crab legs!! Ha! These people didn't know me. They were simply there because I have a degree in selling ice to Eskimos!! So I'm told.

My question to them was always, "What do you think??" The common answer, "They have tremendous promise!! But lady, the name, The Crabb Family, you have to change it!!" There were often a few more comments that I won't repeat.

My answer was always, "No. That's not going to happen. No name change." And for a few years, it bothered me. But now? I laugh. Those folks with the expert opinions?

They never bring it up!! HA!! So, enjoy the cheesecake. And be thankful it's not a seafood dessert!! That would be pretty disgusting.

And these handsome fellows, Eli and Ean Crabb, are proud representatives of the name we didn't change!! And I love them.

CAKE FOR BREAKFAST OATMEAL CAKE

INGREDIENTS

For the CAKE, you will need:
- 1 1/2 cups boiling water
- 1 cup quick oats
- 1/2 cup shortening
- 1 cup brown sugar
- 1 cup white sugar
- 1 1/2 cups all purpose flour
- 2 eggs
- 1 teaspoon baking soda
- 1 teaspoon cinnamon
- 1/2 teaspoon salt

For the ICING, you will need:
- 1 cup sweetened shredded coconut
- 1 cup pecans
- 1 cup brown sugar
- 8 tablespoon melted butter
- 1/2 cup of milk
- 1 teaspoon vanilla

STEPS TO COOK

01. First: Preheat the oven to 350 degrees.
02. Pour boiling water over quick oats, let sit for 20 minutes
03. Combine dry ingredients in a bowl and set aside. In mixer, cream together shortening and both sugars until light and fluffy. Mix in eggs then add dry ingredients. Scrape down the sides of mixing bowl and stir in the oats.

Blend until smooth, but don't over mix the batter. Pour into pan.

<u>SUGGESTED PAN SIZE</u>:
This cake recipe can be made in a well greased 9" x 13" cake pan. . Bake for 30 minutes.
This recipe is a great option for a very large cast iron skillet! Grease the skillet generously with butter.

<u>TO MAKE THE ICING</u>:
01. In a saucepan, combine melted butter, sugar, milk, vanilla, coconut and pecans. Cook topping mixture until sugar is dissolved.

Spread topping on top of cooked cake. Broil until browned.

It's highly likely that by the time you finish reading these stories that accompany my favorite recipes, you will be fasting and praying for me. Some of you will identify, but some of you will be thinking that I need to lay off the sugar and find a NEW hobby. And you are completely correct. Contrary to what some people may say, I do not EAT an entire cake. Sometimes, I take a bite and that's it.

Okay. That happened once. And yes, I do eat cake for breakfast at times. I've done that since I became an adult and could choose what I had for breakfast. Ha!!

Steve has tried to MAKE me like eggs. He cooks them for me most mornings. I don't hate them, but I don't get up thinking, "I am so excited!! I get to eat eggs this morning!"

On the other hand, THIS CAKE THOUGH.

Here I go again, proclaiming my love for ALL things that are akin to a brown sugar based icing. If this were Facebook I would give it a thousand heart emojis!! Honestly, I could face plant in this cake.

This is THAT cake. You get an old beat up pan out, no one to impress here, make the cake. Smell it. Lick the bowl, taste test the icing, about 32 times. Save a little for the cake though.

And then, I cover it and put it up. It ain't beautiful, and you probably won't even post a picture!! But if you wake up at 2 am to go potty (the language of toddlers) you're remembering this cake. It's sending you little shout outs. "I'm here, in the microwave where you hid me. You know I want out of here."

So, I typically oblige, go rescue the cake from the awful perils of being locked in the microwave, and have an obligatory pinch, that turns into a nice big piece.

Then, back to bed. Remembering the plan!!

The next morning:

Steve, "Morning honey. How do you want your eggs today?"

Me, "No eggs for me honey. I'm having an oatmeal thing I made yesterday, the eggs are already in it!!"

#CakeForBreakfast   #DietCokeToo

KATHY'S PINEAPPLE UPSIDE DOWN CAKE

This cake recipe is a great "dressed up" boxed cake mix!

INGREDIENTS

For the CAKE, you will need:
- 2 sticks softened butter (8 ounces)
- Juice from 1 large can of pineapple rings
- 1 teaspoon mayonnaise (heaping)
- 3 eggs
- 1/3 cup sour cream
- 1 box of your favorite yellow cake mix

For the ICING, you will need:
- 1 large can pineapple rings
- 1 1/2 sticks of butter
- 1 box of dark brown sugar
- Maraschino Cherries

STEPS TO COOK

01. Preheat the oven to 350 degrees.

This cake calls to make the icing first, to go in the bottom of your pan! The next step lists ingredients that can be found under the icing list above.

02. In your cast iron skillet melt your butter listed for icing, when it is melted add in the dark brown sugar, stirring thoroughly. Spread mixture evenly in the bottom of the skillet. Arrange pineapple rings in a layer, covering sugar and butter mixture. Place a cherry inside each ring of pineapple. Set your prepared pan aside.

03. In a large mixing bowl combine cake mix, eggs, butter, pineapple juice, mayonnaise and sour cream. Blend until smooth, but don't over mix the batter. Pour into the prepared pan. Your cake batter will be thick, you can shake the pan to even it out or use the back of a spoon.

SUGGESTED PAN SIZE:
This cake is screaming to be made in a well-seasoned cast iron skillet! I recommend a 12" skillet, but any larger size skillet will work, just adjust your bake time accordingly. Bake for approximately 30 minutes. Do NOT overcook! Check every 10 minutes with a toothpick or fork for doneness.

This cake recipe can also be made in a 9" x 13" pan if you do not have a cast iron skillet. But my recommendation is that you go buy one!

TO MAKE THE ICING:
Your icing has already been made and is hiding under that golden brown cake. Now comes the tricky part, turning that heavy cast iron skillet out onto a large platter or plate. When the skillet has cooled slightly, lay your serving plate upside-down on top of the skillet, grasping both tightly, and flip! You may require help for this move, it takes practice! The delicious dark brown sugary topping and pineapple rings will be on display!

Your skillet will stay very warm for a long time, I recommend wearing pot holders! Do not let the cake cool completely, or the topping will stick to the bottom of the pan.

This cake has been a part of my life since before I was. I remember climbing up on the table as a toddler, just to eat the crunchy, heavenly brown sugar icing of this cake, each chunk making me so happy. The topping chunks up, into grainy, candy-like covering, adorned with the roasted pineapple rings. In my opinion, brown sugar and pineapple may be the most PERFECT combination of foods. This topping euphoria is real, folks. If you can make this and not lick the sugary remains from the skillet, you are not human!!! Ha!!

My brother, sisters, mom, dad, AND myself ALL loved this cake so much. It's a pretty big part of my childhood food memories.

We didn't bond a lot over food, at the Jean and Elaine Coppage house. Mom and Dad weren't what we would currently term as foodies. Mom weighed 110 pounds most of her life, Dad topped out at about 145. And then there's me!! My sister often says she married young so she could do as she pleased. When asked what she wanted to do, her answer is always the same. She said, "I wanted to eat honey buns and drink cokes for breakfast!!!!" Ha-Ha!!!

So, our home was a bit like some of the folks in 2020, very portion controlled and health conscious. But there were certain foods that I remember Momma loving so much, that it was totally worth it to her!

No one could make this cake like Momma!!! And today, as I type this, looking at life in the rearview mirror of time, I wish I could revisit that little kitchen. I wish I could sit at that little hard-rock maple table. I wish I could watch her cut me a piece that was SO SMALL it was barely three bites, and I even wish I could hear her say "no more" until tomorrow.

And guess what, Momma was right. I should have saved some for tomorrow...many times.

But the bigger point? The kitchen IS the heart of the home. When we're gone, our recipes, our "food love" that we so generously bestow on our family? It lives on.

Like my momma, I make this cake for my family. My kids LOVE it. The day we shot these photos, they licked the cake plate!!

The sweetest memories I have of Mom and Dad, are memories at the kitchen table. Okay, go make this cake, and I'm going to go have a good cry!!

SUNDAY IN THE SOUTH CHERRY PINEAPPLE DUMP CAKE

This is an easy, delicious cake made from ingredients you likely have on hand. Here in the South, we always like a quick go-to for unexpected guests!

INGREDIENTS

For the CAKE, you will need:
- 1 can cherry pie filling (21 ounces)
- 1 can crushed pineapple (15 ounces)
- 1 1/2 sticks butter
- 1 box of your favorite yellow or white cake mix

You MAY need:
- Whipped Cream
- Ice Cream

STEPS TO COOK

01. Preheat the oven to 350 degrees.
02. Dump pie filling and crushed pineapple into greased 9" x 13" baking dish, stir together. Sprinkle the cake mix over the top. Slice the butter into thin slices; lay slices evenly over the top of the cake mix.

SUGGESTED PAN SIZE:
This cake should be made in a 9" x 13" baking dish. Bake for 45-55 minutes, until the top is brown and bubbly.

This cake is wonderful alone or served along with a scoop of ice cream or whipped cream.

VARIATIONS:
All cherry pie filling, omit the pineapple and add additional cherry filling. You can substitute canned peaches, apple pie filling or blueberry pie filling for the dump cake. Keep the cake mix and butter the same.

Lord have mercy, mention a dump cake, and my mind immediately goes to church homecomings!! My memories go back to our old church in Philpot, Kentucky. Grace Chapel. The birthplace of the singing Crabb Family. And I've included a picture for you. I wanted you to see where it started!! Humble, a bit like the dump-cake. But don't EVER underestimate humble beginnings!!!

It was the textbook potluck kind of church. Outside in the summer, in the fellowship hall when it was a snowy day, as is pictured.

I would have to say I've eaten as much "dinner on the ground" food as anyone on planet earth!! Some of these touring singers say, "I don't eat it, I take it to the bus and pitch it." Well, not this fluffy girl. It's like a casserole and dump cake buffet for me!!

And who doesn't like a casserole or dump cake? You may be from the SOUTH if you'd trade three servings of roasted asparagus for one serving of hash-brown casserole.

Or you may be from the south if you'd trade a raspberry sorbet for a dump cake!!!

If you're the person who bought this book because you love my family's music, yet you had no intention of BAKING any of these cakes. Let's say you simply bought it to support the cause. You always say, "I'm not a cook!!!"

Let granny here challenge you. Let today be the day that changes.

Run out and get the ingredients, take the ten minutes needed to DUMP this cake together, and you will feel so accomplished!!

This cake WILL never fail you. Bake it, put on a favorite Crabb or Bowling record, throw two scoops of ice cream on top while it's still warm, and be ready for one of the best food experiences you've had lately!! And if you're not a southerner? WELCOME to the south. This is how we roll!!!

And what does the underrated dump cake teach us? CAKES do NOT have to be difficult, to be WONDERFUL!!

ADAM'S ANYTHING BUT BASIC WHITE CAKE
(ADAM'S FAVORITE)

This beautiful white cake can be treated as a birthday cake awaiting sprinkles, a wedding cake with beautiful decor or anything in between.

INGREDIENTS

For the CAKE, you will need:
- 1 cup unsalted butter, room temperature (Make sure your butter has no added dye! We want the whitest butter possible.)
- 1 3/4 cups sugar
- 6 large egg whites, room temperature
- 2 3/4 cups all purpose flour
- 2 1/2 teaspoons baking powder
- 1/2 teaspoon salt
- 1 teaspoon almond extract, use a clear one for a whiter cake (Feel free to adjust this amount down to a quarter or half teaspoon if desired.)
- 1 teaspoon vanilla extract, use a clear one for a whiter cake (If you adjust the almond extract down, you can add an additional splash of vanilla.)
- 10 ounces whole milk, room temperature
- 2 ounces vegetable oil

For the ICING, you will need:
- 8 ounces pasteurized egg whites, room temperature
- 7 3/4 cups powdered sugar
- 4 cups of unsalted butter, room temperature
- 1/2 teaspoon salt
- 1 tablespoon vanilla extract, use a clear one for a whiter icing

STEPS TO COOK

01. Preheat the oven to 335 degrees.
02. Beat butter until smooth, slowly add sugar and let cream until light and fluffy. About 5 minutes. In a bowl combine flour, baking powder and salt, set aside. In another bowl combine milk, oil and extracts, set aside. *(See note below) Slowly add liquid egg whites into the mixer, allowing it to slowly and fully combine with your creamed ingredients. (The egg whites being at room temperature is very important! Cold egg whites will curdle your batter.) Add in about one third of your dry ingredients and let combine, then add in half of your wet ingredients. Repeat the process, allowing mixture to just combine after each addition. Blend until smooth, but don't over mix the batter. Pour into pans.

SUGGESTED PAN SIZE:
However, to make a small wedding cake, double the recipe and use the standard three tier.

This cake should be cooled for about ten minutes, then turned out. Wrap tightly, while still warm, with plastic wrap and place in the freezer to flash chill. This will keep moisture in the cake! Once cool, but not frozen, unwrap and trim any brown edges off of the cake.

TO MAKE THE ICING:
01. In a bowl combine egg whites and powdered sugar, whisk on low to combine then switch to high. Add in your vanilla, salt and butter in small chunks. Whip icing on high until light, fluffy and white.

Apply icing to the cake once it is flash cooled in the freezer.
Cake can be stored in a container in the refrigerator for up to three days. This cake is typically gone before then!

*At this step in the instructions you can either follow them as written for a moist, delicious white cake! Or, you can whip your egg whites separately until firm peaks form. After batter is combined and completed, fold in your egg whites gently. This method creates a lighter, more delicate cake but can easily be overmixed.

This is Adam's favorite cake!!! And if I'm being honest, it may be mine as well!! Adam is that guy. He doesn't demand much and is known for his kindness. So that makes it twice as nice to see him dig into something that HE loves!!! This is one of those things. If he comes to a city near you, bring him this amazing cake.... and instruct him to bring me a piece back to Tennessee!!! Ha!! He's such a sweetheart, he'd probably bring me all of it. I love that kid!

When you make this cake, I encourage you to use flowers or fruit to decorate it!! That's what we do. You can turn a summer afternoon into a garden party. Grab a hat, a pitcher of sweet tea, a blanket, and this beautiful little cake, and you're all set!! It's a photo shoot and a cake party!!

That's exactly what this photo depicts. They put flowers on the exact same cake. I love cake cardboard or doilies, it always makes the cake look PRO, even when it's totally not!!

Sometimes, it's the little things. The presentation of a cake with fresh cut flowers is unmatched, in my opinion. A small wedding cake, a birthday cake, this is THE recipe!! SO GOOD!!

45

SOUTHERN ITALIAN CREAM CAKE

This cake recipe is a great "dressed up" boxed cake mix!

INGREDIENTS

For the CAKE, you will need:
- 1/2 cup butter, softened
- 1/2 cup shortening
- 2 cups sugar
- 5 large eggs, separated
- 1 cup buttermilk
- 1 teaspoon vanilla
- 2 cups all-purpose flour
- 1 teaspoon baking soda
- 1 teaspoon salt
- 1 cup shredded or flaked sweetened coconut
- 1 cup chopped pecans

For the ICING, you will need:
- 1 stick butter, softened
- 1 package cream cheese (8 oz.), softened
- 1 teaspoon good vanilla
- 1 pound powdered sugar

You MAY need:
- chopped pecans for garnish

STEPS TO COOK

01. Preheat the oven to 325 degrees.
02. Cream butter, shortening and sugar in a large mixing bowl with an electric mixer. Add egg yolks, one at a time, mixing well after each. Add buttermilk and mix well; add vanilla. Sift flour, baking soda and salt together in a medium bowl; add coconut and pecans and toss together well, then stir into wet ingredients. Mix well by hand. In another bowl, beat egg whites until stiff. Fold gently into cake batter. Blend until smooth, but don't over mix the batter. Pour into pans.

SUGGESTED PAN SIZE:
This cake recipe calls for three 9" round cake pans. Bake for 25-30 minutes.

TO MAKE THE ICING:
01. Cream butter and cream cheese together in a medium bowl; add vanilla, and gradually add powdered sugar, beating until smooth.

Apply icing to the cake once it is cool. Top with nuts for garnish, if desired!

There are a few things that come to mind when I think of a TRUE southern woman. You have a pet word for other women. Like sugar-lump, darling-baby, or honey.

She tells the babies to "give her some sugar" when she wants a good-bye kiss. She also calls her children babies until they're 55, or she's dead, whichever comes first.

A TRUE southern woman, who is over fifty, will twitch when she sees people wear white shoes before Easter, or suede shoes in the summer.

A true southern woman uses y'all in EVERY sentence, will order a sweet-tea and roll her eyes when they tell her it's instant, she's usually a little obsessed with her state, and her favorite response is "BLESS their heart" or the newly learned, shortened version "bless."

And this TRUE SOUTHERN WOMAN....wow, this sister can cook. And to be in this club in a LEGIT way, there are two pre-requisites.

One, she must know how to make enough sausage gravy for the entire men's breakfast at the church. If you can't? You better learn. It's either that or pack your bags, you're moving to the north. Ha!!

Two. She MUST know how to make an Italian Cream Cake!! It's a requirement. From scratch, well iced, and ready to serve on pretty plates, with flowers on the table, alongside a pot of your favorite coffee.

This is the cake you put your BEST foot forward with. Dinner for the pastor, your son's fiancé, a new neighbor who thinks that she's moved to a hick town!!! Ha-ha!!

It's a TRUE taste of the south, and typically prepared by women who have mastered southern cooking, southern living, and most importantly....southern LOVING!!!

Love is a verb you know. In the south we make a cake and invite someone over to share. It feels like love on a fork.

JASON'S FAVORITE CHEESECAKE

INGREDIENTS

For the CRUST, you will need:
- 1 cup graham cracker crumbs
- 1/4 cup light brown sugar
- 1/2 stick unsalted butter, melted

For the FILLING, you will need:
- 12 ounces cream cheese
- 4 ounces sour cream
- 1/4 stick unsalted butter
- 3/4 cup sugar
- 1/2 teaspoon vanilla extract
- 2 eggs

STEPS TO COOK

01. **For the crust:** Preheat the oven to 350 degrees F. Mix together the graham cracker crumbs, sugar and butter, and then spread into a 9-inch pie pan to make the crust. Bake for about 10 minutes, and then let cool.

02. **For the filling:** Mix together the cream cheese, sour cream and butter in a bowl until well blended. Add the sugar, vanilla and eggs and mix well again. Spread the filling on top of the crust. Place the pan in a rectangular baking dish and cover with parchment paper to prevent browning on top. Bake for 45 minutes, and then let cool and refrigerate overnight.

This is one of Jason's favorite desserts!! Krystal makes it for the family, often. Don't make Jason a complicated cheesecake. He will just say, "I'm full!!" He wants plain, New York Style, typically without a topping!!

As I was typing this, and the words jumped at me. Jason. New York. I was reminded of a trip I took with him. You guessed it. To New York City!!

June of 2005. It was a rocky season for me, for all of us I suppose. Life had smacked us around a bit, and the kids needed a break. Adam planned to go to the beach, I think Aaron had planned a trip, and if memory serves me, maybe the girls too. Jason was thinking about getting away, until. We got the call!!

Billy Graham was going to do a New York City crusade!! It was slated for Flushing-Meadows Corona Park, on June 26th. Jason had recorded a song with the Brooklyn Tabernacle Choir, back in April of the same year. I write extensively about that in Stronger.

The Brooklyn Tabernacle Choir had been invited to sing at this history making event!! And as the Lord would allow it to happen, Carol Cymbala, the award winning choir director and the pastor's wife, decided that they needed to sing THAT song at the crusade. Her people called our people to inquire about it. The formal invite came for Jason to sing "I'm Amazed" with the choir!! The music manager in me was jumping for joy, because I KNEW this was historic. But bigger than historic, my heart smiled as I thought about this kid from Beaver Dam, getting to sing his song to 100,000 New Yorkers. I knew that God had arranged this.

So we went. Jason, Crystal Burchette-Johnson, and myself. We got on a Delta flight, and off we went!! Crystal was our publicist, and believe me, that child worked her hiney off for several days in advance of this event!! After we arrived in New York, Ed Leonard joined us as well. He's the president of the record company that had the Crabb Family under contract. We ALL knew that we were blessed to be in that hot muggy city on this particular week.

The weather was blistering hot...in the nineties. We walked the streets of New York and popped into a little restaurant close to Broadway, and yes, we had cheesecake. I had been to New York several times in my life, but never in the heat of the summer. I can't explain how miserable the weather was.

But I also can't explain how worth it, it was.

This proved to be Reverend Graham's last crusade. I love the memory of being on that front row, watching Jason sing his heart out, and Billy Graham preach the unashamed truth of the GOSPEL.

All these years later, I remember the sermon. You see, the backdrop of the week was a bit different for a country girl from Kentucky. The city was immersed in rainbows, scantily dressed men, in women's clothing. It was a lot for me to process.

Reverend Graham had scheduled this last-stand crusade during New York City's Gay Pride March Week. There were two and a half million people in town for the march. The roads were closed, and folks like us had to walk miles upon miles. But hey, we did it. But Graham was in lock step with the dueling agendas. He had 35,000 intercessors in the city that were there to pray!!!

He preached it hot, and it was hot!!!!

He said, "Jesus Christ said, as the days of Noah were, so shall also the coming of the son of man be. When the situation in the world gets the way it was in Noah's day, you can look up and know that Jesus is close to coming."

93 acres of people, and the sermon was being translated in 13 languages. And the WARNING was clear. America? The Lord is coming. You better be ready, because it's looking like Noah Times are on the agenda!

What a day. What a man. The Lord was pleased!! I knew I had witnessed history in the making on that June day!

And while I'm on the subject? I found a photo of a New York trip that Jason and Shellye took, and again they had Junior's cheesecake.

Bonus moment? They met the president.

Let's start eating cheesecake, maybe we too can bump into him.

New York Style CHEESECAKE, for the win!!!!

KATHY'S SWEET POTATO WEDDING CAKE

INGREDIENTS

For the CAKE, you will need:
- 2 1/2 cups all purpose flour
- 2 teaspoons baking soda
- 2 teaspoons baking powder
- 1/4 teaspoon salt
- 2 teaspoons ground cinnamon
- 2 teaspoons ground nutmeg
- 1 cup sugar
- 1 1/2 cups margarine or butter
- 1 cup brown sugar, you can use either dark or light brown
- 3 large eggs
- 1 tablespoon vanilla extract
- 2 1/2 cups mashed cooked sweet potatoes
- 1/2 cup crushed pineapple, drained
- 1 cup raisins
- 1 cup chopped walnuts

For the ICING, you will need:
- 2 blocks of cream cheese, softened (8 ounces each)
- 1/3 cup butter, softened
- 1 tablespoon vanilla extract
- 3 cups powdered sugar

You MAY need:
- Additional toasted walnuts

STEPS TO COOK

01. First: Preheat the oven to 350 degrees.
02. Combine flour, baking soda, baking powder, salt, cinnamon, nutmeg and sugar set aside. Cream together butter and brown sugar on low speed, then increase to medium until well combined. Gradually add the dry ingredients, mixing on low speed until just combined. Add eggs, one at a time beating well after each one. Scrape the sides of the bowl after each egg. Add vanilla, sweet potatoes, pineapple, raisins and walnuts. Mix on low speed until combined. Pour into pans.

<u>**SUGGESTED PAN SIZE**</u>:
This cake recipe calls for two 9" round cake pans. Bake for 50-60 minutes.
You can also use three 8" cake pans.

<u>**TO MAKE THE ICING**</u>:
01. In a bowl, beat cream cheese and butter on medium speed until smooth. Add vanilla and powdered sugar, beat on low speed until combined.

Apply icing to the cake once it is cool. Top with additional toasted walnuts if desired.

The world has changed since the days of the large church weddings of the sixties and seventies. The days of formal receptions being a MUST, are forever gone. Practicality, destination weddings, and the bride and groom being involved in the planning, seems to be here to stay.

Back in the seventies, the norm was a bit different. The bride and her family planned, paid, and the groom showed up!! Or that's how I remember it. Many of my friends had year-long engagements, a five or six tier cake, and hundreds of people squeezed into a church fellowship hall.

I opted for simple, but most southern brides didn't. So, here we are in a world that has relaxed the rules for the "right" way to get married. I watch the social media photos of beautiful back-yard weddings, beach weddings, we've actually had one of those. Adam and Kaitlyn had a beautiful beach wedding a few years ago. Kelly, Krystal, Amanda, Shellye, and Terah...pulled that together for them in days!!

Their wedding is a perfect example of the point I am making. The pictures are the main priority for most couples. The beach, the mountains, a barn with great string lights, a field of flowers, today's brides are looking for the beautiful backdrop. They're not the generation that wants church paneling in their wedding pictures!! Ha!

So, I see and hear of many destination weddings, vows exchanged on a family farm with only the family as guests. I totally understand this!! The people who mean the most? Have them. Utilize the location that feels like YOUR happy place, yes. And some of these younger brides are doing exactly what my girls did. They are leaning on the family members who can pull it together artistically, and also engaging the family member with culinary skills.

A wedding cake for 25 to 50 people doesn't have to be a daunting idea. You should make a practice round, find a technique that you can master, and go for it!! I love flowers, and a naked cake is EASY!!!

The other trend is this. Unusual cake flavors. So I'm whirling a VERY unusual idea at you. A sweet potato WEDDING cake!! I love the unusual, I bet you noticed!!!!

Easy to make, easy to decorate. It is also a fabulous idea for an anniversary cake. These wedding cakes do not take immense decorating skills!!

Girls, we can do this!! Think how special it would be to bake a wedding cake for your grandchild. Naked or fully iced, this cake is delicious!!!

51

THE PEACE CAKE

This is a Southern cake classic! This version is slightly updated, but sure to be a crowd pleaser!

INGREDIENTS

For the CAKE, you will need:
- 3 1/2 cups all purpose flour
- 2 cups sugar
- 2 teaspoons baking powder
- 1 teaspoon kosher salt
- 1 teaspoon ground cinnamon
- 1/2 teaspoon baking soda
- 1/2 teaspoon freshly grated nutmeg
- 1 cup canola or vegetable oil
- 3 large eggs, beaten
- 2 cups ripe, mashed bananas (about 4 bananas)
- 1 small can crushed pineapple with juice (8 ounces)
- 1 tablespoon pure vanilla extract
- 1 cup chopped pecans

For the ICING, you will need:
- 2 packages cream cheese (8 ounce each)
- 2 sticks unsalted butter, softened
- 6 cups powdered sugar
- 2 teaspoons vanilla extract
- 1 cup chopped pecans, toasted

STEPS TO COOK

01. Preheat the oven to 350 degrees.
02. Combine the flour, sugar, salt, baking powder, baking soda, cinnamon, and nutmeg in a bowl and set aside. In a large mixing bowl whisk together the eggs and oil until combined. Add the mashed bananas and crushed pineapple with the juice, stir until combined.
03. Stir the liquid mixture into the dry ingredient mixture with a spatula or wooden spoon, just until combined. Gently fold in pecans and vanilla.

Pour cake batter evenly into prepared pans.

SUGGESTED PAN SIZE:

This cake recipe calls for three prepared 8" or 9" round cake pans. Bake for 25-30 minutes.

TO MAKE THE ICING:
01. Cream the cream cheese and butter until light and fluffy, slowly add the powdered sugar until desired consistency is reached. Beat in the vanilla.

Apply icing to the cake once it is cool. Sprinkle toasted pecans on top.

Cake should be stored in the refrigerator if not eaten within two hours. Take out of the refrigerator one hour prior to serving to bring up to room temperature!

Jesus actually told us to Love our enemies. What?? Explain that please!!

To love our enemies is a totally foreign concept. Love and enemies are words that seem mutually exclusive, at least to me they do. Listen up. I know what it feels like to be mistreated. I also know what it feels like to be bitter for a decade. Who lost? Me.

Now. I am NOT suggesting that you make your ex-husband a cake. I am not suggesting that you make a childhood abuser a cake. That's a bit different. And the RECIPE would be very different!! Ha!!

But what I am suggesting?? If you had a text fight with your sister? Bake her this cake. It's delicious. Just drop it off with a note that says, "I love you." That's it. No rehashing who was right. The truth is? You don't have to be right all the time. There are no scorekeepers, and there are no winners when families fight. Make the cake.

If you have bad feelings toward a friend, a neighbor, a co-worker, I challenge you. Make the cake. Let's start a trend!! Again, no explanation: Just a note that says, "I hope your day is great!"

This cake is divine. And it feels laborious when you're enjoying it. It feels like someone went to TROUBLE to make it!!

About now you're thinking. This is the weirdest cookbook I've ever seen.

Yep!! I think you're right. Now, make the cake!!

THE HANNAH SMORGASTARTA
(SWEDISH SANDWICH CAKE)

INGREDIENTS

- 2 round loaves of bread,* 2 lb (Choose a sturdy bread. Hawaiian round bread can also be used)

For the CREAM CHEESE "FROSTING", you will need:
- 1 lb cream cheese
- ½ c sour cream or plain non-fat yogurt
- 1 tsp ground white pepper
- 1 tsp garlic powder
- ½ tsp salt

FILLING 1, you will need:
- 5 oz smoked salmon
- 1 sliced cucumber

FILLING 1, you will need:
- 3 hard boiled eggs, peeled and sliced
- 1 seedless cucumber, sliced

ALTERNATE FILLING IDEA:
- (3) 6 oz. shrimp salad or tuna salad. Make sure it's not weeping. Liquid isn't your friend when making a sandwich cake.

There is no wrong way to make this. If your family only likes smoked turkey and ham, then that's the ticket. I think it's always nice to add something crunchy, like a cucumber or a bibb lettuce.

Feel free to be creative!!

STEPS TO COOK

Cut the edges from your round loaf to give you 2 inch high sides. Carefully remove the bottom crust and level the top. Slice the round into two even layers. Set the bread layers aside.

01. Make the Cream Cheese "Frosting" by beating together the cream cheese, sour cream, pepper, garlic, and salt using an electric hand mixer. The mixture should be soft and spreadable. Set the "frosting" aside.

MAKE THE CAKE:

01. Place half sheets of parchment paper around the edges of your platter or cake stand to keep the edges clean. Place one of the bread layers over the parchment paper. Lightly spread the bread with a layer of the cream cheese mixture. Over the cream cheese, place a layer of your first filling.
02. Spread a thin layer of the cream cheese mixture over one side of the second bread layer and place that layer, cream cheese side down over the filling layer.
03. Spread a thin layer of cream cheese mixture over the top of that bread layer and cover the cream cheese layer with your second filling,
04. Spread a thin layer of the cream cheese mixture over one side of the third bread layer and place that layer, cream cheese side down over the filling.
05. Now it's time to "frost" your cake. Spread a thin layer of the cream cheese mixture over the top and sides of the cake, using a spatula or cake spatula to spread it smooth.
06. Decorate the cake as desired with vegetable garnishes or smoked salmon, shrimp, or cheese.

The cake can be served immediately or refrigerated, covered, for up to 24 hours before serving.

*Alternately, make this cake rectangular or square by using a pre-sliced loaf of bread. Remove the crust from the slices and layer the slices on a platter to form your desired shape.

And don't we all feel fancy as we read this recipe!!! I have mulled over putting this in the "cakebook" for a week!! I wanted to give a hat-tip to my mother-in-law, and this reminded me of the entire Hannah family!! So, I just had to!! What a fun little project.

Sisters and brothers, let me tell you. All of that wonderful cream cheese, paired with your favorite filling, is crazy good!! They love to come together and bring fabulous finger foods for gatherings. They do the holiday menus too, but I think they enjoy the fun food just as much!!

And somehow, I can see Steve's sisters or his mom creating this, with great patience and design skills!! I am looking for it at the next family gathering!! Ha!

Don't sweat if your family hates seafood. Use turkey and ham. Short of pickled bologna, anything is fine!!! Ha!!

Make one, master it, and then make it for an unsuspecting crowd. THEY are going to be so impressed!! I sure was!!

Serve with a charcuterie board full of your favorites, a fruit tray or a cheesecake, and you are country club material!!!

I want to hear from you when you try this!! I can't wait!

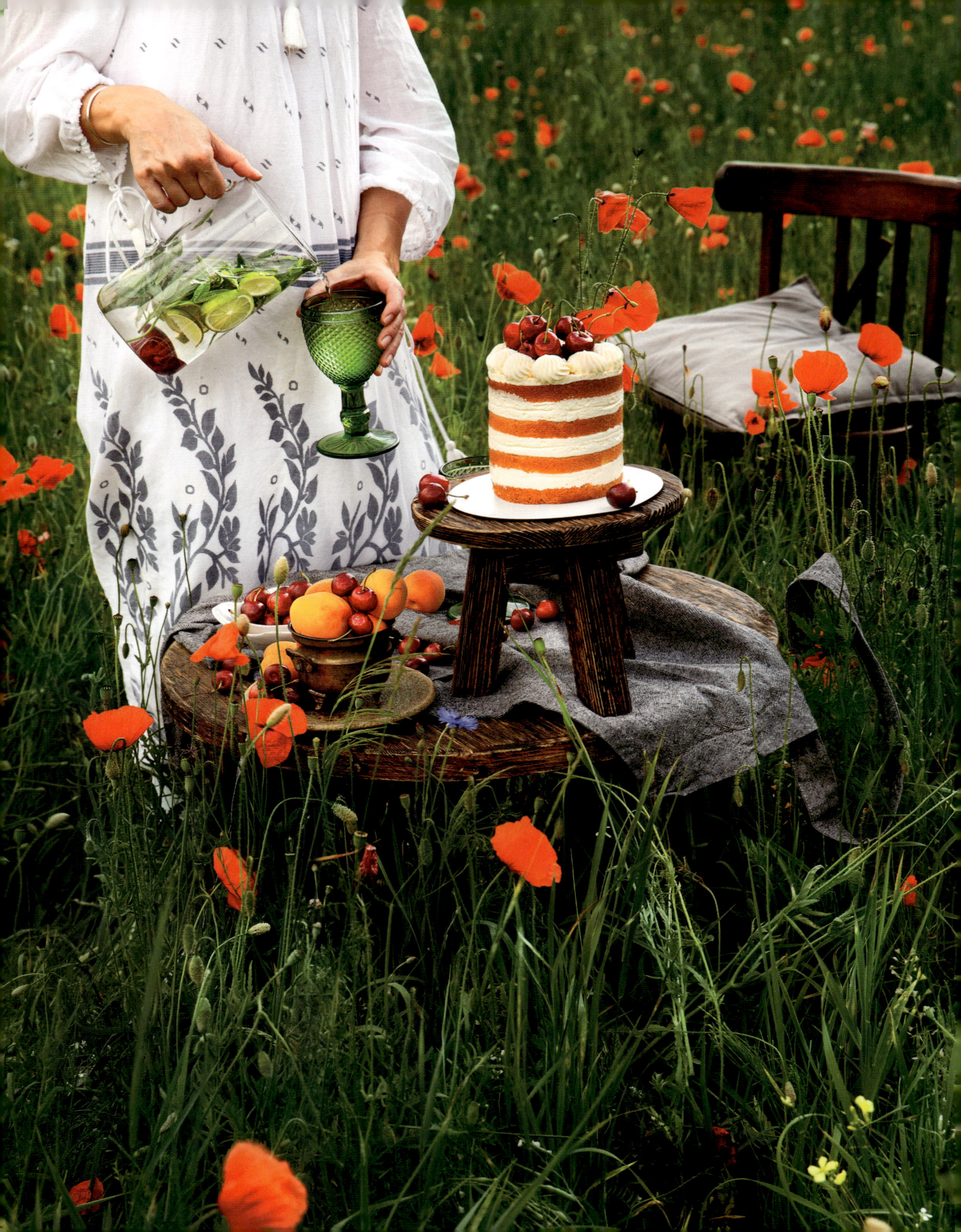

Summer

The days are longer, the hair a bit messier. For the season that gives permission to indulge is here. We suddenly have permission to sleep a bit later, or use that credit card, without guilt, to book the beach trip we so need.

Summertime is interchangeable with chill-time, in my mind. I recall long, sweet days of banana ice cream churning…..as we cranked an old wooden freezer, or ate a ripe watermelon while lying on a hand-made quilt…..that quilt ALWAYS smelled like pure sunshine. It had been dried on a clothes-line by the sun and the wind. How I miss that!

When I smell a blanket that has that sunshine smell, or Copper-Tan suntan oil, or the amazing smell of a steak that's sizzling on a grill? It's officially summertime!!

The berries are riper, the butter is sweeter, the kids are hungrier, and the laughter is louder. Summer is here.

Enjoy the sunshine and laughter!! Store up the joy, take pictures, write stories, especially of funny grandkid moments. Your 80 year-old self will thank you.

I watched my momma's life shrink from a house full of furniture, junk for days, a couple of cars in the driveway, and a busy social life well into her eighties.

She was able, until she wasn't. Oh my, it happened fast. She lived on pictures and memories, as will most of us.

At the end? We took home a little box of items from the nursing home…as they took her body away in a hearse. I cherish that little box. We come here with nothing, and we take nothing when we go. But between the dashes on the obituary, there's a lot of summers to enjoy.

So love your life. Take it as it comes. You've weathered many storms. Granted. So let's never waste a sunny day, OR a piece of CAKE!

Bake the cake and take the picture. It's what happy people do.

BANANA SPLIT CAKE

INGREDIENTS

For the CAKE, you will need:
- 7 ripe bananas (not overripe though)
- 1 1/2 quarts of strawberries
- 1 can pineapple chunks
- 5 cups confectioners sugar
- 1 block of creamed cheese
- 1 teaspoon vanilla
- ½ cup sour cream
- 3 cups of graham cracker crumbs, crushed fine
- 3 sticks of butter
- 3 tablespoons sugar.
- 1 ½ large containers of Cool-Whip

You MAY need:
- ½ cup milk or whipping cream
- 1 small jar maraschino cherries

STEPS TO COOK

01. Choose your container. I often use a large 10" trifle bowl for this dessert. The layers scream summer, and it's beautiful to see.

    If you don't have a flat bottom trifle bowl, you can use a 15" by 10" glass casserole dish. That works fine.

02. In your microwave, melt 2 ½ sticks of butter, add the 3 tablespoons sugar to your graham cracker crumbs, and start working the crumbs into the butter. I do this by hand. Flatten and shape. If you need additional butter, add it. If you need crumbs, add. This will vary based on pan size and personal preference. There is no wrong way to do this!

    Remember, the crust will be visible.

03. Make your filling. The consistency should be that of a TOO thick cake icing. If it's runny, thicken it. If it can't be managed with a spoon, thin it.

    Combine 5 cups of confectioner's sugar, cream cheese, a stick of melted butter, ½ cup sour cream. Blend with the mixer. It should be thick!! If it's not thick enough, add more confectioners sugar. It it's too thick, add whipping cream or milk, as needed to arrive at the correct consistency.

    Pour filling onto graham cracker crust.

04. Next, drain ALL of the liquid from the pineapple. I actually squeeze each chunk to reduce the liquidity. Arrange evenly on filling.

05. Next, slice about seven bananas for the next layer. The last fruit layer is strawberries. I typically load this dessert up with strawberries. My recipe calls for twice as many as most. However, they are pretty, and doubling the amount will make the dessert tall enough to use that trifle bowl!! Cap them and half them.

    Reserve a half dozen for the garnish on top.

Last, PILE the Cool-Whip on!!!! Add strawberries for garnish, or maraschino cherries I use strawberries because the cherries bleed onto the Cool-Whip. Just a tip!! This dessert will serve 20 to 30 people!!

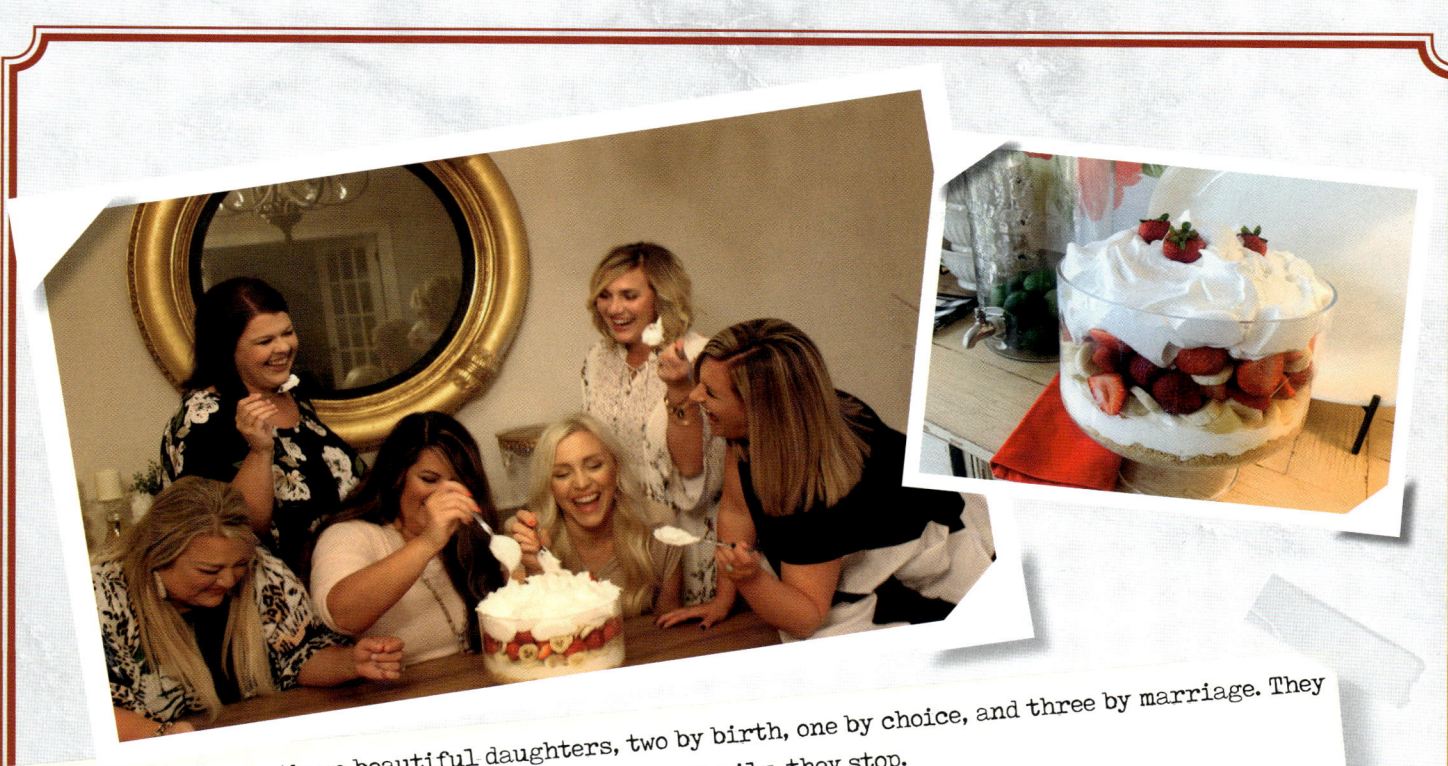

I am blessed to have three beautiful daughters, two by birth, one by choice, and three by marriage. They lead very busy lives. But when it's time to stop and be family, they stop.

After my dad died, my family crumbled a bit. We never got that something back after his death. Mom was different. She was weaker and so lost. She became a widow in her early forties, and it was truly awful. She should have demanded that the family gather. Often, she didn't demand. We gathered less and less. And honestly, my kids don't have many memories of Christmases at her house. She loved us more than life, but she was often FRUSTRATED with less than perfect circumstances, and a bit afraid of being told no. Remember, for every married child you have, you're a mother-in-law to someone.

I learned early in life that the BEST of families fall into a trap. The gatherings will dissipate over time, with the exception of funerals and an occasional "death bed" hospital visit. If we don't put the time into planning and CREATING an environment of family, it's over.

I vowed to NEVER allow this to happen. I will find a reason! It's typically centered around food and music! And yes, we ARE a blended family. And the fact that we're still a FAMILY, is nothing short of a miracle. Look at GOD! Our family chose love, about fifteen years ago...when the tie that bound ALL of us together, untied himself.

That's cookbook code for we got divorced. Ha!! But through it all, the dinners kept happening, the celebrations, the birthdays, the happy family moments...that would prove to undergird MY grandchildren with a sense of belonging. Those moments became sweeter than ever. Because we had CHOSEN each other based on time spent, love, and a true sense of "we meant it when we said we were a family."

As I type, I'm thankful for the support these girls give me, and each other. They love each other. Shellye has been here since she was sixteen, Amanda was nineteen when Aaron met her. I've had these girls for over half of their lives. The point? It takes work and commitment to stay involved and connected. But it is so worth it!! Most people that I meet struggle with this!! My advice? Make this luscious dessert and INSIST that the family come over and partake!! Give everyone a spoon, and tell them to dig in. Real family will eat from the bowl!!! Ha!!

59

STRAWBERRY CAKE

This cake recipe is another great "dressed up" boxed cake mix!

INGREDIENTS

For the CAKE, you will need:
- 1 cup canola oil
- 1/2 cup of buttermilk or whole milk
- 4 eggs slightly beaten
- 3 ounce box of strawberry Jell-o
- 1 cup of fresh strawberries mashed or finely chopped. (If you can't find fresh, frozen will work.)
- 1 box of your favorite white cake mix

For the ICING, you will need:
- (1) 8 ounce cream cheese at room temperature
- 1/2 cup butter at room temperature
- 5-6 cups of powdered sugar
- 2 tablespoons heavy cream

You MAY need:
- 1/4 cup fresh strawberries drained after being mashed
- 2-3 drops red food coloring

STEPS TO COOK

01. Preheat the oven to 350 degrees.
02. Combine cake mix and Jell-O in a large mixing bowl. Slowly mix in the eggs, milk. and oil stirring gently between each item. Stir in strawberries. Mix for about 3 minutes, scraping down the bowl several times. Pour batter in selected pans.

SUGGESTED PAN SIZE:
This recipe recommends a well greased 9"x 13" cake pan. Bake for 38-30 minutes.
You could always use 8" or 9" round or layer pans, also. Just adjust your baking times accordingly.

TO MAKE THE ICING:
01. Blend cream cheese and butter until smooth. Sift powdered sugar and add one cup at a time to creamed ingredients. Blending sugar into the mixture until smooth. Add heavy cream as needed until desired consistency is reached.
02. Add strawberries and food coloring if desired.
03. Apply icing evenly to the cake once it is cool.

Strawberries!!! Is there anyone who doesn't love them?? My goodness, my entire family is crazy about this cake. If you have a friend who can decorate, this is the cake to call in the favor for!!!

Cream cheese icing, and those beautiful strawberries resting on top like a crown on a queen!! Truly, if the world of cakes was ruled by a monarchy, this would be the queen!!

Addi, my little great-granddaughter, refuses chocolate and ALWAYS asks for strawberry anything. Cake, ice cream, whatever. I have tried to talk her down occasionally when I ran out of strawberry ice cream. You know...that old "EVERYONE loves chocolate" line. Her response would be, "Give me vanilla with strawberries on top." That smart little cookie!! So I am known to keep strawberries in season, and strawberry ice cream at all times, almost. Truly, my family eats the berries out of the bowl, standing at the kitchen sink!!

Amanda is allergic to chocolate, so I always try to have a strawberry alternative for parties. Well, Addi is on the Amanda train. Don't be bringing her no chocolate cake!!! Strawberry all the way!!!

This cake is absolutely divine!! I've never met a human that didn't love it!!! If you don't like it, please don't EVER TELL me!! Ha!

Let me live in my world of strawberry cake perfection. Yes, this cake is perfection!!

I encourage you to ice it pretty. Not everyone can call in a friend to swirl it and curl it, but you can take your time and make it your own!! This queen deserves it.

My cousin Dinah gave me this recipe, and it's the best STRAWBERRY CAKE recipe in the south!! Thank you Dinah!!!

THE HAPPY CAKE

This cake recipe is a great "dressed up" boxed cake mix!

INGREDIENTS

For the CAKE, you will need:
- Cooking spray
- 3 (18.25 ounce) packages white cake mix
- 9 large egg whites egg whites
- 4 cups water
- 1 cup applesauce
- 2 (16 ounce) cans white frosting
- ½ fluid ounce red gel food coloring, or as desired
- ½ fluid ounce orange gel food coloring, or as desired
- ½ fluid ounce yellow gel food coloring, or as desired
- ½ fluid ounce green gel food coloring, or as desired
- ½ fluid ounce blue gel food coloring, or as desired
- ½ fluid ounce purple gel food coloring, or as desired

STEPS TO COOK

01. Preheat the oven to 350 degrees F (175 degrees C). Spray two 9-inch cake pans with cooking spray.

02. Combine cake mix, egg whites, water, and applesauce in a large bowl using an electric mixer. Divide batter evenly into 6 bowls. Mix a different food coloring gel into each bowl. Pour the red batter and orange batter separately into the prepared cake pans.

03. Bake in the preheated oven until a toothpick inserted into the center of each cake comes out clean, 25 to 30 minutes.

04. Remove from the oven and let rest on a cooling rack in the pans for 15 minutes. Flip quickly onto the rack and remove cakes from the pans. Continue the baking and cooling process with remaining batter until all layers are cooled.

05. Shave off the tops of the cakes carefully using a large knife so they will be flat. Place the red layer down, frost the top lightly; continue with orange, yellow, green, blue, and purple.

06. Frost the top and outside of the cake. Cut through using a big, sharp knife and serve.

We made these in mini pans too,
and garnished with fruit!!! So cute for a party!!

This cake is absolutely beautiful!! It's like HAPPY on a plate. Maybe it's the child in me, but all of those colors make me light up like a Christmas tree!!!

Someone once told me, "Count your rainbows, not your thunderstorms."

As I've poured out my love in this book, you've gotten a little piece of my heart. I have been a fixture in a little grandma chair in my upstairs office for days. I've been hashing through recipes, memories, and re-tracing many life experiences, trying to vividly recall a specific taste as I remember the gatherings that reminded me of the HAPPY rainbow days.

And yes, I am trying to minimize the thunderstorm days.

No one wants a thunderstorm cake, after all!!! Ha!!

It's a bit overused I suppose, but I surely don't care. I will say it anyway. I'm old and I'm a bit overused as well I suppose.

But the truth is this. There's ALWAYS, ALWAYS something to be thankful for. And I've commonly observed as I've trudged through this messy life of mine...thankful people are happy people.

I've known people who lived in a shack, they didn't have ten dollars in the bank, yet they could sing "Tis So Sweet, To Trust In Jesus.....Just to take HIM at His word!!!"

Tears falling, an old broken down table in the kitchen, not a matching chair at the table. And yet? The joy of the Lord....was as thick as molasses in that home. Well, glory. I'm feeling this as I type.

And then? I must tell you. I know people who God has clearly blessed with everything. I mean everything. And they're empty, searching, and live like a dog chasing a car. Like the dog, they will never catch the car. Dogs don't catch cars.

And the sad part?? The car chasing Christian truly loves God too. But somehow, in the midst of the busy life of success and prosperity, they have forgotten that being thankful is more than giving to the poor. It's more than saying a bedtime prayer. One is required to STOP, and let our heart get involved.

So today I challenge you. Stop. Allow yourself the luxury of telling the LORD what you're thankful for.

Be happy. Eat HAPPY cake, and tell someone you appreciate them!!

GOLDIE'S SUNSHINE CAKE

This cake recipe is a great "dressed up" boxed cake mix!

INGREDIENTS

For the CAKE, you will need:
- 1 can mandarin oranges, not drained (11 ounces)
- 1/2 cup vegetable oil
- 4 eggs
- 1 box of your favorite yellow cake mix

For the ICING, you will need:
- 1 can crushed pineapple, not drained (20 ounces)
- 1 tablespoon sugar
- 1 package Jell-O cheesecake filling mix (10 1/2 ounces)
- 1 container of Cool Whip topping (9 ounces)
- 1 container of sour cream (8 ounces)

STEPS TO COOK

01. Preheat the oven to 325 degrees.

02. Beat cake mix, eggs, oil and undrained oranges. Blend until smooth, but don't over mix the batter. Spoon batter evenly into pans.

SUGGESTED PAN SIZE:
This cake recipe calls for two well greased 9" round cake pans. Bake for 30 minutes, or until a toothpick comes out clean.

TO MAKE THE ICING:

01. In a bowl, combine pineapple, sugar, cheesecake filling mix and sour cream. Stir until mixture thickens. Fold in whipped topping, mixing thoroughly..

02. Apply icing to the cake once it is cool.

Cake can be stored in a container in the refrigerator for up to three days. This cake is typically gone before then!

If you're making this for a party, I recommend that you make two of these and make them three layers each. That would simply mean you double the recipe!!

The process of putting together this cakebook has been a bit like a stroll through the memories that are lurking in the unused portion of my mind. When I started remembering these cakes, the folks that shared the recipes so generously, the memories have been plentiful, and in living color!

This recipe is Goldie Payne's. We've been friends for forty years. I can barely say that. It almost chokes me. It feels like we should be celebrating our 35th birthday, but no. I'm barreling toward my 65th like a locomotive headed down a hill.

Goldie is a sister music chick. I first heard of her WAY back in my early twenties I think. She was a local celebrity of sorts in the Owensboro, Kentucky area. She was an on-air personality at the big 100,000 watt country station, WBKR, and everyone knew Goldie. Well, they thought they knew her. After all, EVERYONE listened to the radio back in the seventies. No cell phones, no streaming, no cable in our neck of the woods. There were three television stations, and there was WBKR. I'm not big on secular music these days. I simply don't have time for it.

But listen here, sister here can sing you EVERY lyric to a Ronnie Milsap hit, an Alabama hit, and Reba, Dolly, or Ricky. The early songs. Those lyrics are locked away in the backroom of my memory, JUST WAITING for that melody to perk up my ears.

The ears alert the "song memory room" and just like that!!! I'm wailing, singing a very questionable harmony part, but doing my best to make them proud!! Ha!!

So my point, I knew Goldie, but she certainly didn't know me. One day I read a newspaper story. It announced that Goldie was opening an "Opry House" in Owensboro. A country music show with a spattering of gospel, EVERY week!! How exciting. It was called "Goldie's Best Little Opryhouse in Kentucky." Goldie is a great singer, and she has more charisma than a televangelist!!

I was a music lover. I played piano for a local group of close friends. Those of you who know me, you know that my motto is, "YOU have not, because YOU ask not."

So guess who faniggled around until she got Goldie's number? Yep!! I called and chatted, and she booked us. This is the first stage that Kelly ever sang on!!

So here we are forty years later, two old Kentucky girls, still loving music, baking cakes, trusting Jesus, taking trips together, and meeting every now and then for dinner!!

I love Goldie, and I sure do love this cake!!

As a bonus I dug up some old photos and a newspaper clipping. Kelly's first singing appearance at "Goldie's Best Little Opry House" and a newspaper clipping from the following year!!

OREO ICE CREAM CAKE
AN ORIGINAL FROM KATHY

INGREDIENTS

For the CAKE, you will need:
- Two packages of Oreos
- Two sticks of butter
- Two half gallons of vanilla ice cream
- Four tablespoons Hershey's chocolate syrup

You MAY need:
- Peanut butter chips

STEPS TO COOK

01. First, take your ice cream out of the freezer for 30 to 45 minutes. Depending on the temperature in the room. You will allow it to thaw until you can easily work it like cookie batter.

Take about 48 Oreos, put them in a large freezer bag, crush with a hammer. Do not use a food processor. The cookies should be fine enough to use for a crust. You want to know it's an Oreo, yet be able to blend with butter. Take your cookies, add warm melted butter, and form a crust. This is similar to the process for a graham cracker crust, but we're using Oreos instead.

Pack the crust in your 9" by 13" glass pan, or an 11" or 12" round bowl. I often use a heavy, large bowl that has a flat bottom. It's transparent, and the dessert is pretty when viewed from the side. A trifle bowl is fine as well, if it's VERY large. If you're entertaining and want to look a bit fancier, do the round!!

After you pack your crust, work your ice cream on top. Smooth it and top with more Oreo crumbs for a garnish. Drizzle the chocolate syrup to your desired taste, and re-freeze the entire thing for an hour!!!

For a "moose tracks" taste, add peanut butter chips if desired.

This is SUCH a simple summer treat. My family loves it!!

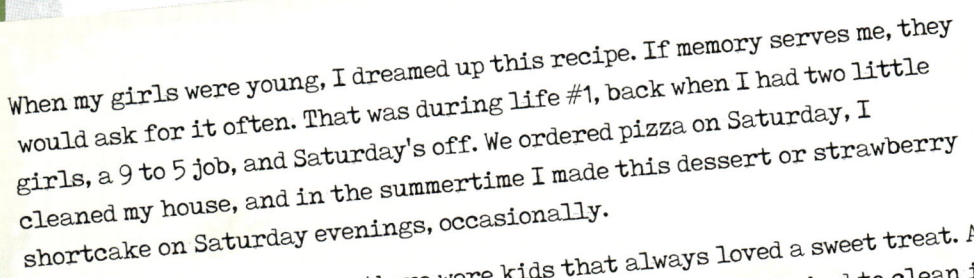

When my girls were young, I dreamed up this recipe. If memory serves me, they would ask for it often. That was during life #1, back when I had two little girls, a 9 to 5 job, and Saturday's off. We ordered pizza on Saturday, I cleaned my house, and in the summertime I made this dessert or strawberry shortcake on Saturday evenings, occasionally.

My family lived nearby, so there were kids that always loved a sweet treat. And then, life happened. I got a better job. I no longer cleaned house on Saturdays, my girls had to clean it, or I hired someone to help. Time became the one thing I had very little of. We transitioned, a lot, as a family. My normal became a lot of carry-out food, and a season of never enough time.

And then I re-married, the Crabb Family musical touring entity was birthed, and I was BUSY for the next twenty-five years. I forgot about this dessert!! Last year on Mother's Day I was trying to think of something new to add to Krystal's meal she was preparing for the entire family. I needed a dessert to feed an army. However, I didn't want to bake. After all, it was Mother's Day weekend!!! I thought I should wear my crown and get a pedicure, as opposed to slaving in the kitchen!! Ha!!

While some lovely gentleman was rubbing my old woman feet, I REMEMBERED this little secret. The OREO ice cream cake!!! That's it. I ordered the ingredients while he was painting my toes. It was waiting on my porch when I returned to my house. The ice cream was perfect for the prep!! A bit squishy just like it needs to be!!

And the next day, it was a hit. I will quote Hope. She said, "And WHERE has this been all of my life? I'm nineteen and I've never had this!!!"

And truly it made me realize that our busy years become busy decades. And sometimes it's necessary to stop and remember what we loved back then....because our grandkids will love it now!!

Like, fresh-squeezed lemonade, hand churned banana ice cream, snow cream, or a coke float. When's the last time you made something that you loved many years ago, but haven't had in decades??

Maybe today is the day. And this little ice cream cake?? Try it. It's a winner.

REPUBLICAN RED VELVET CAKE

INGREDIENTS

For the CAKE, you will need:
- 2 cups sugar
- 2 eggs, room temperature
- 3/4 cup vegetable oil
- 1/4 cup butter, melted
- 1 cup buttermilk, room temperature
- 2 cups cake flour
- 1 teaspoon salt
- 1 teaspoon baking soda
- 1 teaspoon baking powder
- 2 teaspoons vanilla
- 2-3 tablespoons unsweetened cocoa powder
- 1 tablespoon vinegar
- 1/2 cup black coffee
- 2 ounces red cake color

For the ICING, you will need:
- 4 blocks of cream cheese, softened
- 2 sticks butter, softened
- 1 box powdered sugar, plus a bit more if needed
- 2 teaspoons vanilla

STEPS TO COOK

01. Preheat the oven to 325 degrees.
02. Stir together flour, baking soda, baking powder, cocoa and salt. Set aside. In a mixing bowl combine oil and sugar, blend in the buttermilk, eggs, vanilla and food coloring. Stir in the coffee and white vinegar. Mix the dry ingredients into the wet ingredients, a small amount at a time. Blend until smooth, but don't over mix the batter. Batter will be thin. Pour into pans.

SUGGESTED PAN SIZE:
This cake recipe calls for two prepared 9" round cake pans. Bake for 30-40 minutes. Do not overbake! You could also use a 9" x 13" cake pan, or a bundt cake pan. Adjust time accordingly.

TO MAKE THE ICING:
01. In a bowl, combine cream cheese and butter. Beat until smooth. Add sugar and vanilla, mixing well. Spread between layers and ice cake thoroughly with mixture. Adjust consistency with additional sugar as needed.

This recipe makes a LOT of icing! You can easily use it for a 3 layered cake. If you are making a 9" x 13" or bundt cake, you can cut this recipe in half.

My Granddaughter, Cameron, and I at the 2016 presidential inaugural ball

Okay, you know you laughed a little bit when you saw the name of this cake!! Then, you read the ingredients, and thought it was very much like a RED velvet cake!! Yep!! You are so right. But I am typing this note 80 days before the 2020 election. And it's my book, so I can name it anything I please!! Ha-ha!!!

And this sister is a political creature!! I feel that silence is often sin. Elections for me are typically about life. The varied issues impact me, but nothing impacts me like a vote to protect the most vulnerable among us, the babies!!

The heartbeat of my life has always been my children and grandchildren. By default, the Republican Party gets my vote!! And of course, I live in a VERY RED state.

I propose a resolution that would make THIS beautiful cake, the official cake of the Republican Party!! As soon as I finish typing, I'm texting the president and suggesting this idea!! HA!!!

I have an idea!! Every time I see a red velvet cake being served, I am going to say, "Did you know this is President Trump's favorite cake? We even re-named it the Republican cake."

And who knows?? Maybe I will end up with an extra piece of cake every now and then. You know how partisan people are about our president!!

So be it!!! An extra slice of cake is always a blessing, no matter how it's obtained!!

Enjoy!!! If you're a Democrat and offended by my little note, feel free to send me your slice!!

MOMMA'S 7UP CAKE

This cake recipe is a great "dressed up" boxed cake mix!
It will take you back to simpler times.

INGREDIENTS

For the CAKE, you will need:
- 3/4 cup vegetable oil
- 10 ounces 7Up
- 4 eggs
- 1 box of your favorite lemon cake mix
- 1 small box pineapple instant pudding mix

For the ICING, you will need:
- 1 bag of sweetened shredded coconut
- 1 1/2 cups sugar
- 1 stick margarine or butter
- 2 eggs
- 1 small can crushed pineapple

STEPS TO COOK

01. Preheat the oven to 350 degrees.
02. Stir together cake mix and pudding, blend well. Add in oil, 7Up and eggs. Blend until smooth, but don't over mix the batter. Pour into pans.

<u>SUGGESTED PAN SIZE</u>:
This cake recipe calls for three 9" round cake pans. However, we made it in a bundt pan!! Bake for 25-30 minutes.

<u>TO MAKE THE ICING</u>:
First: In a saucepan combine coconut, sugar, butter, eggs and pineapple. Cook over medium heat until thick. Spread between layers and on top of the cake.

Apply icing to the cake once it is cool.

Cake can be stored in a container in the refrigerator for up to three days. This cake is typically gone before then!

When we made this cake, we omitted the pineapple and coconut. We drizzled the icing and added lemons!!

And you can make the icing completely optional if you like!!

Once again, I have a lemon cake!! As I told you in another cake note, I learned to love lemons as an adult. But my little momma made this cake, when I was a child!! It reminded her of summer. I didn't appreciate the cake then, and by the way, she did the luscious icing when she baked it. But I appreciate it now!!!

NOTHING wakes up your taste buds like something sour and sweet, in one bite! We did the lemons on top for the sake of photography, but the icing is truly divine.

As I think of the simple times of my childhood, and then parallel that era to the world that my grandbabies are living in?

It makes me feel like the recipes weirdly connect the generations. Nothing else is the same. iPhones have replaced eight party lines. Computers have replaced encyclopedias. The old Sears and Roebuck Catalog has been replaced by Amazon.

But here's the truth!! Nothing will ever replace a scrumptious cake that's baked with LOVE by a momma or granny!!! And to have these recipes that have been tested and loved, is such a BLESSING!!

If you can convey that cooking is a form of giving, to your daughters and granddaughters, it will serve them!! Cooking doesn't have to be beneath the station, it doesn't mean we're less than intellectual or incapable of a career. You know my opinion on that. I believe that GIRLS can do anything!!

But truly, cooking is like hugging. It's the outward display of what's in our heart!!

So, cook with your girls, show them how rather than telling them how!!! It may prove to be the love language around your home!! I love it when my babies come visit me and we cook!!! These girls are amazing. I am blessed and I know it!!

PISTACHIO HEAVEN CAKE

This cake recipe is a great "dressed up" boxed cake mix!

INGREDIENTS

For the CAKE, you will need:
- 1 box pistachio instant pudding
- 1 cup of club soda
- 3 eggs
- 1 cup of oil
- 1/2 cup of chopped pecans
- 1 box of your favorite yellow cake mix

For the ICING, you will need:
- 1 box of pistachio instant pudding
- 1 1/2 cups of milk
- 2 cups thawed Cool Whip

STEPS TO COOK

01. Preheat oven to 350 degrees.
02. Beat cake mix, pudding mix, eggs, club soda, oil and chopped pecans for about 2 minutes on medium speed. I always mix the dry pudding into the dry cake mix prior to adding the wet ingredients to help prevent any clumps of pudding mix.

    Blend until smooth, but don't over mix the batter. Pour batter into your prepared pan.

SUGGESTED PAN SIZE:
- This cake recipe calls for greased 9" x 13" cake pan. Bake for about 30-35 minutes or until golden brown.

    You could also use a very well greased bundt cake pan for this recipe. I always use butter to grease my pans. If you make the bundt cake, you will need to bake it for about 50-55 minutes.

TO BLEND THE ICING:
01. In a bowl, combine pudding mix, thawed Cool Whip and milk. Mix for about 2 minutes until well blended.
02. Spread icing on cooled cake.

Daddy loved pistachio pudding, airplanes, and his kids. The fact that he was a type 1 diabetic proved to be enough of a problem that he curtailed the sweets, on most days. He died at 50, and somehow, that's been 50 plus years ago. Wow, time? Where did you go? And yes, he died loving airplanes, family, and anything sweet!!

When I try and remember his likes, his dislikes, I find that the memories are faded. And it makes me cry. But one random memory is I faintly remember Daddy loving this green pistachio pudding.

I'm a bit weird about colors and food. I don't do blue drinks, they remind me of the Ty-D-Bol in our toilets when I was a child. I also don't do two white starches together on a plate. My momma shamed us for that. Ha-ha!! Remember, she had a 19-inch waist!

She thought potatoes and macaroni and cheese, together, would be a sure ticket to Weight Watchers, or possibly hell, I'm not sure which. And she declared that WE DON'T do that around here!!! We have a green vegetable, a yellow, a nice pop of red on that plate, and VERY little WHITE!! So, I am clearly jaded when it comes to the color of food. I wonder how many of you are?

I typically love a color that suits my preconceived idea of the CORRECT color for a cake. You know, chocolate icing, or creamy white with a half pint of sliced strawberries on top, and the occasional cake that feels like fall. Maybe a spice cake with a rich caramel colored icing running down into the grooves of the cake plate. That's my cake norm.

All you folks that have weird FOOD color issues, don't be judging this little WINNER by the green color!!

My old friend Debbie...makes this cake and it's DIVINE!!! Debbie has been my friend for fifty years. She's a southern girl, and knows a good recipe when she finds one!!

You need to make this cake, invite a friend over and have a little back-yard dinner party!! Pair it with Rosemary chicken, squash casserole, a cute little green salad with heirloom tomatoes, and a BIG glass of sweet tea.

And that my friends, is how we do it in down south!! And notice that I was careful with the colors on my plate of my imaginary meal that I prepared for the back-yard dinner party!!!!

73

LUSCIOUS LEMON CAKE

When life gives you lemons, make a lemon CAKE!!

INGREDIENTS

For the CAKE, you will need:
- 2 1/2 cups of all purpose flour
- 1 3/4 teaspoons baking powder
- 1/4 teaspoon baking soda
- 1/2 teaspoon salt
- 1/2 cup unsalted butter at room temperature
- 1/2 cup vegetable oil
- 1 1/2 cups sugar
- 1/2 teaspoon vanilla extract
- 4 eggs
- 3/4 cup milk
- 1/2 cup fresh lemon juice
- 2 tablespoons fresh lemon zest
- 2 tablespoons poppy seeds

For the ICING, you will need:
- 2 8-ounce packages of cream cheese at room temperature
- 3/4 cup of butter at room temperature
- 10 cups of powdered sugar
- 1 tablespoon of fresh lemon juice
- 1 tablespoon of fresh lemon zest

STEPS TO COOK

01. Preheat oven to 350 degrees.
02. Combine the flour, baking powder, baking soda and salt in a medium sized bowl and set aside.
03. In a bowl, cream the butter, oil, sugar and vanilla extract and beat until light and fluffy, about 3 minutes.
04. Beat in the eggs, one at a time. Once eggs are added, scrape down mixing bowl.
05. Add half of the dry ingredients, just until combined.
06. Mix the milk and lemon juice together, then slowly add the mixture to the batter. Mix until combined but do not over mix the batter.
07. Add remaining dry ingredients and mix until combined. Scrape down the mixing bowl to be sure the ingredients are combined.
08. Add the lemon zest and poppy seeds to the batter, stir until combined.

<u>SUGGESTED PAN SIZE:</u>
- This cake recipe calls for three 9" round cake pans. Bake for 22-25 minutes.

<u>TO BLEND THE ICING:</u>
01. In a bowl, combine cream cheese and butter and beat until smooth.
02. Add half the powdered sugar and mix until combined.
03. Add the lemon juice and zest and mix well.
04. Add the remaining powdered sugar and mix until smooth.

As always with cream cheese icing: if it's too thick? Thin with warm butter, one teaspoon at a time.
A little bit goes a long way with powdered sugar.

Apply icing to the layers of the cake once it is cool.

I became addicted to lemon desserts after I turned fifty or so. What a late bloomer I am!!!

When I was a child, Momma made lemon pies that were awful, and I think it ruined me. Let me explain. Dad was a type 1 diabetic, and our kitchen ALWAYS had a tall bottle of saccharin on the counter, right beside that old copper-tone stove-top. This was before Sweet 'N Low, Splenda, and Equal. It was also before fast-food and quick anything. Bless my momma's heart, she tried. She made desserts for Dad, and used that GOD AWFUL stuff. Yuck!! I haven't seen a bottle of that in years. I suppose they don't make it anymore. That's the good news of the DAY!! No more liquid saccharin.

Anyway, Momma made these horrible chocolate and lemon pies with that awful stuff. They would nearly gag me. So I checked lemon desserts OFF MY LIST for about forty-five years.

But holy cow!! For the love of ALL things sugary and sour at THE SAME TIME!! One day? When I was well past fifty, someone brought me a lemon cake. It was moist, dense, and drizzled with sugary wonderfulness. I was going through a TERRIBLE divorce. And the truth is? I ate it for breakfast for a week. I often quote, When life gives you lemons, MAKE A LEMON CAKE!!

My friend Laura makes this cake! And it's beyond GOOD!! If you're having a LEMONY day!! Make this cake! And invite me over!!

SOUTHERN STRAWBERRY SHORTCAKE

INGREDIENTS

For the CAKE, you will need:
- 1/2 cup butter softened
- 1 cup granulated sugar
- 1/2 cup buttermilk
- 2 eggs
- 1 teaspoon vanilla
- 1 1/2 cups all purpose flour
- 1/2 teaspoon salt
- 2 teaspoons baking powder

STEPS TO COOK

STEPS TO COOK:
- Preheat the oven to 350, and lightly grease an 8x8 pan or 10 spaces on a muffin tin.
- Cream the butter and sugar with a spoon, beating well until the mixture is light and slightly fluffy. About 40 strokes around the bowl or so.
- Add the buttermilk, eggs and vanilla and mix well.
- Using a sifter sitting over the bowl, add the flour, salt, and baking powder to the sifter and tap the dry ingredients into the wet ones.
- Mix with a spoon until no dry clumps of flour remain.
- Bake 25-30 minutes for the 8x8 pan or 15-20 minutes for the muffin tin until the cake springs back and a toothpick inserted in the center comes out clean.

WHIPPED CREAM TOPPING:
- 1 cup heavy whipping cream
- 2 tablespoons powdered sugar, sifted
- ½ teaspoon vanilla extract

Combine all ingredients in a bowl and whip with a whisk or hand mixer until stiff peaks form.

Arrange in layers on the plate if desired!! Serve slightly warm with fresh strawberries.

ENJOY!

Okay. We're back to strawberries, southern women, and all things good....with this little "from scratch" recipe!

My old friend Melinda sent me this. She's part of my tribe of southern sisters!!

Let's talk about that for a minute. What is a TRUE southern woman?

There's actually about three categories I think. First off, there's the redneck-woman version of the southern woman. Remember the song?

I'm a redneck woman I ain't no high class broad, I'm just a product of my raising, I say, 'hey y'all' and 'yee-haw, and I keep my Christmas lights on, on my front porch all year long...and now you're singing it!!

I don't think that one's me!! Ha!!

And then there's the SPOILED southern girl. Driving the Mercedes, worrying more about her eyelashes than her IQ, and making every man in the state feel inferior to Daddy's money.

Uhm. That was never me either. I love all of these girls, no dissing or anything. But it's just not who WE are.

As I ponder on my idea of a TRUE southern woman...that fits into my group of women, I have my own list of qualifications. Here goes!! Ha!!

One of the requirements is that you know how to bake a cake from scratch. This little cake is a good starting point if you've never. And yes, MAKE the whipped cream too!!

We southern women don't cut corners. You tell us you need to borrow a cup of sugar? We bring the 10 pound bag. You ask for an opinion on your current romance?? We send you a 3,000 word text, links to at least five articles on how to choose the right man, and then we apologize if we stepped over the line!! Ha!!

We stay up later than everyone else, we work a little harder, and we will beat the holy plaster out of anyone who abuses or uses someone we love.

And one more thing about the TRUE southern sister; She cries when she sees the flag, cries harder when someone is baptized, and can forevermore rock those grandbabies to sleep.

We're not the beer drinker, or the spoiled little rich girl, but we're that one in the middle...that's a sucker for a monogrammed anything!! Ha!! We are eternal optimists, and we love a red lipstick.

But the truth is this. Good women, be they from the north, south, east, or west. They stop when another woman falls. They help them dust off their crown, and put it back on them straight.

We're all different. Sure, we have our tribe, our clan of comfort. But God help us to never forget that we must lift each other up.

The prostitute is my sister. The missionary is my sister. The black woman, the red woman, the yellow woman, and the pasty white woman, are all my SISTERS. We stand, often united by a little nuance like a cake recipe.

Let's love one another. For the LORD said to have faith, hope, and love. But the GREATEST is always ♡ love.

And speaking of love. Ain't my grandbabies cute??

JON'S CRAB CAKES

INGREDIENTS

You will need:
- 1 pound fresh or canned crabmeat, drained, flaked and cartilage removed
- 2 to 2-1/2 cups soft bread crumbs
- 1 large egg, beaten
- 3/4 cup mayonnaise
- 1/3 cup each chopped celery, green pepper, red pepper and onion
- 1 tablespoon seafood seasoning
- 1 tablespoon minced fresh parsley
- 2 teaspoons lemon juice
- 1 teaspoon Worcestershiresauce
- 1 teaspoon prepared mustard
- 1/4 teaspoon pepper
- 1/8 teaspoon hot pepper sauce
- 2 to 4 tablespoons vegetable oil, optional
- Lemon wedges, optional

STEPS TO COOK

I recommend a cast iron skillet!!

In a large bowl, combine the crab, bread crumbs, egg, mayonnaise, vegetables and seasonings. Shape into 8 patties. On medium heat, cook patties in a cast-iron or other ovenproof skillet in oil for 4 minutes on each side or until golden brown. If desired, serve with lemon.

Freeze option: Freeze cooled crab cakes in freezer containers, separating layers with waxed paper.
If desired, whip up a quick remoulade sauce!! I think it's a must for crab cakes!!

HERE'S AN EASY RECIPE!!

- 1 cup mayonnaise
- 3 Tbsp. Creole Mustard (or spicy brown grain mustard)
- 1 Tbsp. lemon juice
- 1 Tbsp. Louisiana hot sauce (or your favorite hot sauce)
- 1/3 tsp. garlic, minced
- 1/2 tsp. black pepper freshly cracked
- 1/4 cup dill relish
- 3 Tbsp. ketchup
- 3 tsp. Creole seasoning

I know it's a bit intimidating to make something you've never made!! But you can do it!!

As I was thinking about the recipes for this "cake" book, I immediately knew I wanted my Mom's banana cake, a recipe from my Aunt Net, a few from here, a few from there. And then one night it hit me!!

There's more to life than sugar. There are other yummy food items that are termed as cakes. I immediately thought of crab cakes. How can you not?? Ha!!

And because my girls were involved in the tasting and the photos, I wanted to somehow pay tribute to the sons and sons-in-law. I thought it through. Mike can give me a recipe, so can Brian. They cook a lot. I know that Adam and Aaron definitely have a sweet tooth for the right dessert, and Jason does too. And Jon, yes.... he likes a sweet.

But when I think of Jon, I don't think of a cake, or a cookie. I think of delectable food. As Hope would say, boujee food. You see Jon drove a bus for many years for some of the biggest stars in the world. Those stars stay at 5 star hotels, and the drivers do as well. So Jon-boy has ordered up many great meals from a master chef's kitchen!! He's not easy to impress. Ha!!

I've been contemplating him for a few days. And today, as I was looking for a photo, I saw their wedding pictures. We have one of the entire family!! It's a village. And I said to myself, "That boy sure did get a whole bunch of Crabbs when he decided to marry Terah!!"

And it hit me. I need to put a crab-cake recipe in this book and name it for Jon!! And yes, Jon is from Maryland, so it's SO fitting!!

So here it is kids. I love this recipe!! It's a bit of a grocery trip to find the crab, usually. And I haven't made it during this pandemic where I'm actually not shopping. But I encourage you to make this, at least once!!! Pair it with a beautiful heirloom tomato salad, lemon grilled asparagus, and a few rosemary potatoes!!

And if you make that meal?? You will thank me!!! So good!!

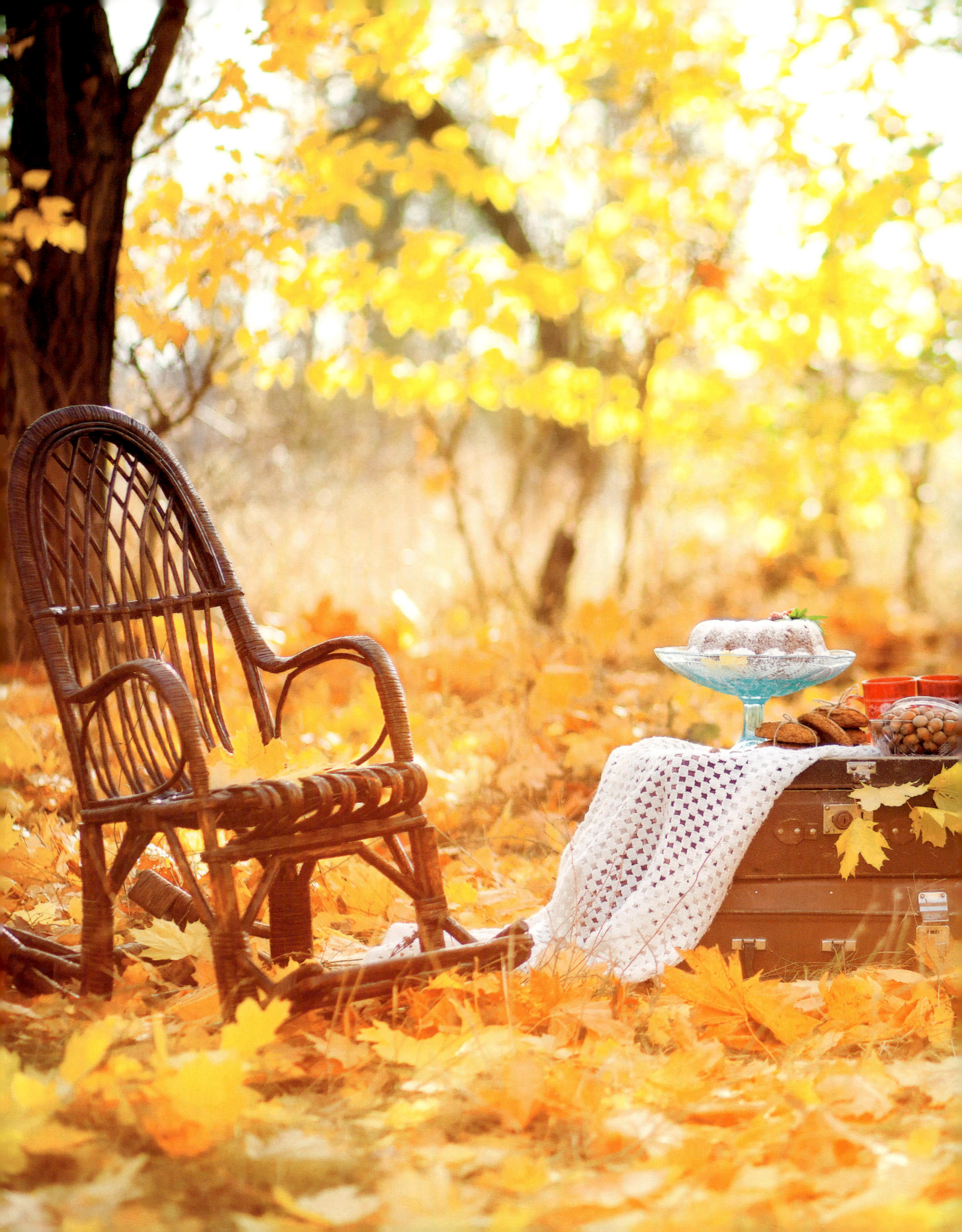

Autumn

As I pondered on which season is my very favorite? It looks like we have a winner! I'm the girl who complains about the weather, 300 days a year. But the 65 that I don't complain? Most are autumn days.

Autumn is like an old friend. Familiar, yet never OVERLY harsh, and somehow comforting……with her smells of spice, warm hues of gold, orange, and rich purples.

I get excited when I see folks bring out their oldest plaid shirt. In the south, the football talk starts, and the pumpkin-spice frenzy begins. The world becomes a great big ball of pumpkin spice, for exactly 54 days.

And then boom, just like that, those pumpkins are in the garbage can, the cute little buffalo check pillows that say "It's Fall Ya'll" be gone to the storage closet. Because you are ditching FALL for Christmas!! In a New York Minute you will be on that train!! You will post, "Is it wrong to put my Christmas tree up in October? ASKING for a friend."

You ain't asking for a friend. You're one of those. You're doing it. And that's okay. You will still love the crisp feeling that's in the air, no worries. Get on with the Jesus party early!! I'm all for it!!

But, for the sake of powdered sugar and all things sweet, don't ditch the fall desserts!! They are TRULY my FAVORITES!!

Now. Let's go bake something!!!

AUNT NET'S OCTOBER CAKE

INGREDIENTS

For the CAKE, you will need:
- One box of yellow cake mix
- 4 eggs
- 1 cup oil
- 1 cup of applesauce
- 1 cup oatmeal old-fashioned oats
- 1 cup brown sugar
- 1 teaspoon cinnamon
- 2 teaspoons vanilla flavoring

STEPS TO COOK

Mix ingredients well, pour into a 9" by 13" pan, two small loaf pans, two round cake pans, or bundt pan, depending on your intent to ice, or not ice. Aunt Net serves this without icing!! It is AMAZING!! Ice and garnish as desired.

But I also love the pairing it with cream cheese icing, or a drizzle. All three options are delish!

Here are recipes for both!

For the cream cheese ICING, you will need:
- 2 blocks of cream cheese, softened (8 ounces each)
- 1/3 cup butter, softened
- 1 tablespoon vanilla extract
- 3 cups powdered sugar

Soften cheese and butter, blend until smooth.

For the drizzle ICING you will need:

- 2 cups powdered sugar
- 1/4 cup butter (4 tablespoons, melted)
- 2 to 4 tablespoons milk (or hot water, for desired consistency)
- 1 1/2 teaspoons vanilla extract
- Melt butter and blend. Drizzle as desired.

When I look at these pictures, it's immediately October and I'm in the mountains, well....at least in my mind. I go back to family trips, grandbabies on the rides, the family singing on a Dollywood stage. And then there's the trip we took when Katelanne was turning one. We rented a HUGE cabin, and celebrated a special time of homecoming with Terah, Jon, and Logan. And little Katelanne, her first birthday party there in that big cabin.

That seems like several lives ago. A lot has changed in sixteen years. And yet, nothing has changed.

The mountains are synonymous with fall, for me. Everything smells better there, tastes better there, and there's just something about the clear-headed thoughts that seem to come easier when the backdrop is the purple hues of those mountains.

I am ALWAYS reminded that God was here a long time before I was. The vastness of Mount Le Conte takes my breath away. Yeah, I know, I know, those mountains are TINY when compared to the Rockies. But hey, it's all about perspective. Compared to the tiny hills around Nashville, the Smokies are daunting and beautiful.

I have thousands of mountain stories. That's a separate book that I'm tempted to write.

But when my mind co-mingles mountain stories and cake equally, I go to the lodge at Hidden Mountain. The cake contests that we've had at our Stronger retreats come to mind. I remember one night. Krystal, Amanda, Terah and Kelly were preparing to minister to several hundred women. The lodge is gorgeous with a huge fireplace as a centered backdrop. I was tired, fried-in-the-brain kind of tired. I had asked God many questions on this day. I felt used up, fed up, and I told God so!!

Have you ever coordinated an event? I'm fairly sure that these are common tendencies for the "day of" meltdown. I was there. I stayed in a different cabin than the girls. So I hadn't really seen them. In passing I said, "What are you all doing tonight?" They were completely in charge of the evening service. They said, "You will see. It's going to be refreshing for everyone." I knew that I SURE needed to be refreshed.

Service time came, and I came in right at starting time. And what did I see sitting in on a stand in front of the fireplace, in the area where the singers were singing? A BOWL of oil. It looked like cooking oil, or olive oil. We are Pentecostal, so oil is common, but this was a LOT of oil.

They sang, praised, but it didn't take long for their "refreshing" plan to start. They anointed EVERY SINGLE one of those women. It took hours upon hours. They prayed for every single need that was represented among them. ONE AT A TIME! Kelly and Terah anointed their hands, Krystal and Amanda anointed their feet. I've never seen anything quite like that night. If you were there, you will never forget. And this isn't the place to go into detail. But my, my!! What a time!!

We weren't in a church, but a lodge, on a mountain, with a cake buffet set up on the porch. The truth is this. When we seek Him, He shows up. When we go to the mountains, it's typically a "seeking" kind of trip. And my word in Heaven, He DOES not disappoint!!

Make this cake. As you add the oil, tell yourself that no one knows the cost of the oil in YOUR alabaster box!!! No one but you and GOD!!

And then do a little praise break in the kitchen!!! Why? Cause you're still able to bake, you're in your right mind, and what tried to kill you only made you stronger!

BETTY'S FAMOUS SHEET CAKE

INGREDIENTS

For the CAKE, you will need:
- 2 cups of all purpose flour
- 2 cups of sugar
- 1 cup of butter
- 1 cup of water
- 4 tablespoons of cocoa
- 1/2 cup of buttermilk
- 2 eggs
- 1 teaspoon baking soda
- 1 teaspoon baking powder
- 1 teaspoon vanilla

For the ICING, you will need:
- 1 box of powdered sugar
- 1/2 cup of butter
- 4 tablespoons of cocoa
- 5 tablespoons of milk

You MAY need:
- 1/2 cup chopped nuts of your choice

STEPS TO COOK

01. Preheat the oven to 400 degrees.
02. Place your sugar and flour in the mixing bowl.
03. In a saucepan add butter, water and cocoa. Bring to a boil and boil for 1 minute. Time this, it will make a difference in your cake. Pour the boiling mixture over your sugar and flour and mix well. Scrape down the sides and bottom of your mixing bowl.
04. Add buttermilk, eggs, baking soda, baking powder and vanilla.
    Blend until smooth, but don't over mix the batter. This is a thin cake batter, so don't be alarmed!
    Pour into your prepared pan.

SUGGESTED PAN SIZE:
This cake recipe calls for a sheet pan, it is technically a half-sheet pan. The kind you use to bake cookies on. Bake for 12-16 minutes.
The cake will be a thin sheet, if your pan or oven is not level, rotate the cake pan halfway through baking.

TO MAKE THE ICING:
You will want to make this icing while your cake is baking, so it is ready when the cake comes out of the oven. First: In a saucepan, bring butter, cocoa and milk almost to a boil (but do not boil!). Remove from heat and add powdered sugar, vanilla and nuts if you are using them.

At times, powdered sugar can create lumps in your icing. Some people say humidity can affect this, here in the South that is a daily battle! Sifting your sugar prior to adding will help to create a smooth icing. If you still have small lumps of powdered sugar in your icing, use a few drops of milk or heavy cream and continue to stir vigorously over low heat until dissolved.

Apply icing to the cake while it is warm.

My dad passed away suddenly when I was only thirteen. Our lives were less than ideal before he passed, but after he was gone, the only normal I knew was completely gone. My parents were good people, but their relationship wasn't stellar. Read my other books for more info. I won't bore you with the sordid details in a cakebook!!

Time passed, and I found myself married at seventeen. I was no more than a confused child, and the groom was a bit older, but we were both kids! He was an older man at nineteen. Ha!! It was Kentucky, and it was the seventies. So, don't judge!!

Fifteen years, two daughters, and a dozen failed attempts to make it work didn't fix it. And yes, we found ourselves divorced.

I often say that I got the sweetest deal from this marriage. I got my beautiful girls, and I got more than a decade of cooking lessons from my mother-in-law, Betty May. When I married her son, I couldn't make macaroni and cheese. But back in those days, we ate at home. Someone once said that I married her son so that I could have a seat at her dinner table!! Ha!! I won't deny or confirm that. But I sure had many meals with her, stalked her in the kitchen, and today, at 64, I still remember so much of what I learned. If you eat my country cooking and like it, say "thank you Betty" as you inhale those mashed potatoes with cream and butter!

The woman could cook. ANYTHING. She made bread daily. She could throw down for a dozen farm hands, or have an afternoon ladies tea, with china and sterling that was fit for the president. I see her in my girls. They love china and a beautiful table. That's the Betty May in them!!

This cake is legendary in the family. Krystal still makes it, and my word, they devour it. I love the photo I'm sharing in this book. It's Betty's great-granddaughters, Eden, Cameron, and Hope, enjoying her cooking legacy. It doesn't get much sweeter than that.

CLARA'S CALIFORNIA ORANGE CAKE

INGREDIENTS

For the CAKE, you will need:
- 1 pound of candied orange slices
- 2 cups of sugar
- 2 1/2 cups all purpose flour
- 4 eggs
- 2 cups chopped dates
- 2 sticks margarine or butter
- 1 teaspoon baking soda
- 1 teaspoon baking powder
- 1 teaspoon salt
- 1 cup coconut
- 1 cup walnuts
- 1 1/2 cups buttermilk

For the ICING, you will need:
- 1 small frozen orange juice
- 1 box of powdered sugar

STEPS TO COOK

01. Preheat the oven to 350 degrees.
02. Combine flour, baking soda, baking powder and salt, set aside.

Cream together sugar and butter until fluffy, add eggs, mixing well. Add flour mixture and buttermilk, alternating and beginning and ending with the dry ingredients. Blend until smooth, but don't over mix the batter. Scrape down the sides of the bowl. Stir in orange slices, dates, coconut and walnuts. Pour into the prepared pan.

SUGGESTED PAN SIZE:
This cake recipe calls for a well greased and floured bundt cake pan. Bake for 50-60 minutes.

TO MAKE THE ICING:
01. In a bowl, combine slightly thawed orange juice and sugar. Mix thoroughly.

Apply icing to the cake while it is still warm.

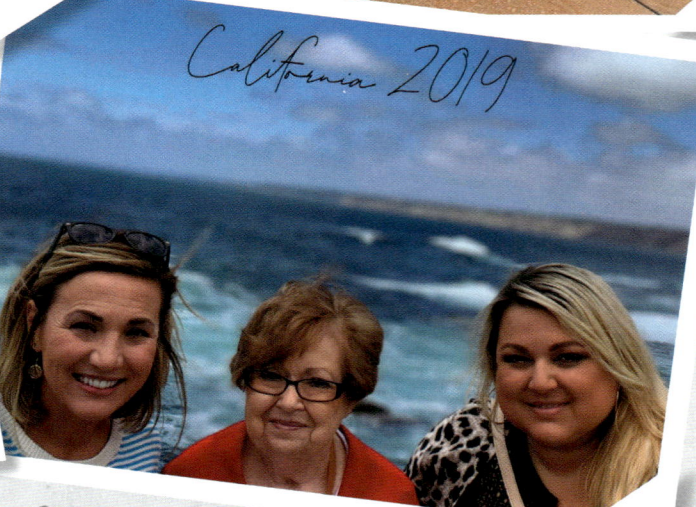

My friend Karen sent me this recipe!! It's amazing. A bit more intense than an orange juice cake, but so WORTH trying! Karen's grandmother Clara made this, and passed this recipe on to her. Karen is an old friend. I met her back in 2004 I think. She won a Christian talent contest at TBN. She's one of those people. When she walks up to the microphone, you know who is in charge. Nope. Not Karen, just Jesus!! And that is why I love her!!

If you read these little stories and laugh a bit, that's good. If you read them and think, "Why?" Thanks for asking!!

Most of us have lived through some messy times. I often say, "You can't unscramble eggs." And yes, about now I'm enjoying my cooking quotes. They fit right in this book.

I have tried to unscramble eggs many, many times. It can't be done! Some things are permanent; The loss of a child, the loss of a marriage, molestation, financial devastation, to name a few.

I've known hundreds of women who have been molested by their fathers. Remember, I'm in women's ministry. I know stuff. People tell me things that they've never told anyone.

I've known hundreds of women who have buried a child. Heavy stuff for a cookbook, huh? Sorry about that. I also know THOUSANDS of women who are estranged from their children. The mental anguish crushes them!!

You can't put the eggs back in the shell, but you can use those messy eggs!!

As we age, we start to understand.

We realize that life TRULY is short. AND we must use our stories to encourage someone else. Last year I decided that a yearly trip with my girls would be healing for all. You see...our lives haven't been perfect. I've damaged them with my choices. You probably have damaged your kids too, truth be told.

Consider this trip idea. Take the trip, eat the cake, and laugh...without the grandkids, without the husbands. Find the dynamic of their childhood, and spend a week. It's healing!! Terah couldn't go, so we took my sister in her place. What memories!!

Daughters and moms, find your peace, find your happy. Allow the past to be the past, and allow God to be who He says He is.

If you're reading this and you feel like it's only you? It's not. We all feel it at times. Inadequate. And what if the reason I felt so compelled to write my random stories in a cookbook, was because GOD knew you would need to read this. Now. What if it's all for you?

What if? Call your estranged daughter or son. Text, e-mail, heck...pull up in their driveway. Tell them you have a cake to deliver.

Be sure you take forks too. You're going to eat that cake with those wayward kids.

I believe!!

SUGAR AND SPICE APPLESAUCE CAKE

INGREDIENTS

For the CAKE, you will need:

- 3 cups all purpose flour
- 2 teaspoons baking powder
- 2 teaspoons baking soda
- 2 teaspoons nutmeg
- 2 teaspoons allspice
- 1 teaspoon cloves
- 2 teaspoons cinnamon
- 1 cup butter, softened
- 1 cup sugar
- 1 cup light brown sugar
- 2 eggs, beaten
- 2 cups applesauce
- 1 cup nuts, chopped
- 1 cup jam or preserves of your choice (use one cup of additional applesauce as substitute if desired)

You MAY need:

- Powdered sugar or Whipped Topping Or a NOT SO SWEET basic cream cheese icing
- 8 ounces cream cheese, at room temperature
- 8 tablespoon lightly salted or unsalted butter, at room temperature
- 1 cup powdered sugar
- ½ teaspoon vanilla extract
- 1/8 teaspoon salt if using unsalted butter
- a squeeze of lemon juice, optional

STEPS TO COOK

01. Preheat the oven to 300 degrees,

02. Cream butter and sugars until light and fluffy, add lightly beaten eggs and jam. Scrape down the sides and bottom of the bowl. Combine all dry ingredients, except baking soda. Add dry ingredients into the wet mix, and mix well. Dissolve baking soda in applesauce, then add applesauce to the batter mixture. Stir in raisins, dates and nuts. Blend until smooth, but don't over mix the batter. Pour into pans.

<u>**SUGGESTED PAN SIZE**</u>:
This cake recipe calls for a large prepared tube pan. Bake for approximately 60 minutes.

<u>**TO MAKE THE ICING**</u>:
Cake can be dusted with powdered sugar if desired. Or, serve alongside a heaping pile of whipped topping, homemade whipped cream, or cream cheese icing!

However, I used this for a birthday cake. You can do three 8" pans and ice as desired!! I like the cream cheese recipe that's included.

Oh my goodness!!! These pictures should make you want to bake this cake!! Everything that makes me smile, everything that I have been blessed with, is easily spotted in these photos.

A lifetime of living, sprinkled with a lot of bumps, bruises, and no one could believe it moments. As a teenager I was attacked in a dark parking lot. I was left for dead after a stranger cut my throat. I didn't die, clearly. But it took 43 stitches to stitch me up. And it took decades of pep talks, just me and Jesus talks, to overcome my fears. Life has had some real moments. I've cried all night during many seasons of life. It was often too painful to talk about, so I sucked it up, slapped on some red lipstick, and smiled. You've done it too. I waited until everyone else was asleep, and then I cried, and ate cake. The struggle is real.

And then there's this. I've celebrated HUNDREDS of birthdays with my babies. I've laughed until I hurt. I've seen the sun set over the beach a hundred times. I've had more kisses than anyone alive today. I've celebrated a passel of healthy grandkids, and I've been known to carry birthday candles and matches in my purse, just in case we do a random birthday party on demand!! Not even kidding.

And EVERY SINGLE time I see a baby's eyes light up with the surprise of a cake? No words.

Life isn't easy for most of us. But I would walk through all of the STRUGGLES again, for this ONE picture on this ONE day!!!

In the end. God is good. Cake is good. And the grandkids are EVERYTHING!

Make the cake and count YOUR blessings!!

AARON'S CARAMEL CAKE

INGREDIENTS

For the CAKE, you will need:
- 1 cup butter
- 2 cups of sugar
- 4 eggs
- 3 cups self rising flour
- 1 cup buttermilk
- 2 teaspoons vanilla

For the ICING, you will need:
- 6 tablespoons butter
- 3/4 cup brown sugar
- 1 tablespoon flour
- Pinch of salt
- 6 tablespoons cream
- 1 cup powdered sugar
- 1 tablespoon vanilla

STEPS TO COOK

01. Preheat the oven to 350 degrees.
02. Cream butter until light and fluffy then add sugar. Cream for about 8 more minutes. Don't skimp on the time! Add eggs, one at a time, and mix well after each one. Scrape down the sides and bottom of the bowl. Add flour and buttermilk, alternately, beginning and ending with the flour. Stir in vanilla, blend until smooth, but don't over mix the batter. Pour into pans.

<u>**SUGGESTED PAN SIZE**</u>:
This cake recipe calls for three 9" round cake pans. Bake for 25-30 minutes.

<u>**TO MAKE THE ICING**</u>:
01. In a saucepan heat butter, brown sugar, flour and salt over low heat. Boil for one minute. Remove from heat and blend in cream, remove from heat and blend in powdered sugar in small increments. Add vanilla and beat until thick, adjusting with additional sugar and cream as needed. Continue to beat icing to desired consistency.

Warm icing can be poured over cake layers. Apply as a more traditional icing once it is cool.

I top with apples occasionally. It's also a great cake to be creative with fall topping choices. Cinnamon sticks are nice too!!

My boys are thin, not the biggest of eaters on most days. They're clearly from a different gene pool. Tall and thin, nope. Didn't get it from me!!

When Aaron was a kid, we would be getting ready for bed on the bus, and I would ask him, "Did you eat?"

He would say, "Oh no. I forgot!!! All I've had is chips today!!!" And one of us girls would say, "How do you FORGET to eat? I wish I could forget!!!"

But everyone has something that they would walk a mile for. With Aaron, it's good Mexican food, a bag of chips, or a GREAT cake!! He does love an occasional sweet!!

And the directions to this cake SO remind me of him. It says "don't skimp on the time." It's crazy how well that sums up Aaron's personality. He's patient, longsuffering, and I don't think anyone has EVER accused him of skimping on the time.

I've been around the world with this kid, who is now my pastor, and I've never seen him put himself before another human. Period. So I can't think of anyone I would rather cook for. My labor is my love. My food is my heart!!

Caramel is one of Aaron's favorites. And this cake is AMAZING!!

As I said, Aaron is my pastor, and everyone knows that we should feed the man of God first. Remember Elijah and the little woman with the meal and the oil in the Old Testament?

So, how fitting for ANY pastor. Make a cake. Deliver it!! And pray a blessing on him as he eats and enjoys. People are hard. Pastoring is hard. Especially in the days we live in. Aaron stands for truth. Sometimes the world doesn't want truth.

Cake is necessary sometimes. Ha!!

Aaron and I have bonded over many things down through time. Mickey Mouse, politics, and yes...a good piece of caramel cake!!!

Bake it. And then invite us over!!

BROTHERS FOREVER CHOCOLATE CHIP POUND CAKE

This cake recipe is another great "dressed up" boxed cake mix! This is a moist, dense chocolate cake! It is wonderful on it's own or served warm with ice cream, coffee or strawberries!

INGREDIENTS

For the CAKE, you will need:
- 1 small package chocolate instant pudding
- 1 container sour cream (8 ounces)
- 1/3 cup of water
- 3/4 cup of oil
- 4 eggs at room temperature
- 2 teaspoons vanilla
- 1 box of your favorite butter cake mix
- 1 cup semi-sweet chocolate chips, frozen

STEPS TO COOK

01. Preheat the oven to 325 degrees.
02. Combine cake mix and pudding in a mixer bowl. Mix in eggs, water, oil, sour cream and vanilla. Mix until well combined, about 3-4 minutes.
    Blend until smooth, but don't over mix the batter. Pour into well greased pan.

SUGGESTED PAN SIZE:

This cake recipe calls for a well greased large loaf pan. The one I use is a Wilton loaf pan, it is 16" x 4". Bake for 55-60 minutes.

You could use two standard loaf pans, or several mini pans. Adjust the bake time accordingly for your pan size.

Once the cake is cool, turn out onto a rack until completely cooled. While still warm, you can top with additional chocolate chips as desired.

This cake title? It's an old Crabb Family song that was written for Adam, Aaron, and Jason. They sang it when they were young, and they cringe when someone plays it!! Ha!! I think it's great, but you know how critical most of us can be when it's OUR teenage photos. We laugh at our hairstyles, clothing disasters, and what have you.

So, they do a bit of the "oh my word, why did I wear that" when we play those old videos. But there's nothing sweeter, at least to me, than a walk down memory lane.

And their walk as brothers...it's a been a sweet one. Adam and Aaron are twins, and Jason is only two and a half years older. So they've walked the road together.

I have involved the girls in the making of this book. It's a girl project I suppose. The daughters, grand-daughters, and even the two great-granddaughters. But when I think about the grandsons, when I think about their delight when these guys see cake?? How can I not?

Charlee is headed into high-school, Ethan first grade, and Grayson is two.

But bring out a hot, chocolate cake, and all three are interested in that!! No matter the age difference, brothers are brothers. My sister is 14 years older than me. But it makes no difference, we're SISTERS.

And these boys? They are blessed to have each other! When they hit adulthood, they will be so thankful for the tie of a brother. That's how it was for me!! My sister became a friend, not a babysitter!! Ha!!

Today, their commonality may be Disney, cake, and cheeseburgers. But one day they will stand on a platform together, make decisions together, and be that friend who you call in the middle of the night.

I often say that cousins are our first friends, but for kids with siblings, that's not really true. Your brother or sister is that FIRST TRUE friend.

As I type this the theme of this book seems to be resoundingly clear. Appreciate family, enjoy your cake, and thank GOD for both!!

As Momma used to say: Don't let the sun sink on your anger. If you're not in a good place with family? Your siblings? Fix it.

Because, we truly are in this life thing together.

#BrothersAndSistersForever

PERFECT PEANUT BUTTER CAKE

This cake recipe is a great "dressed up" boxed cake mix!

INGREDIENTS

For the CAKE, you will need:
- 1 cup butter, room temperature
- 1 cup light brown sugar
- 1/2 cup sugar
- 1 cup smooth peanut butter
- 1 teaspoon vanilla extract
- 3 large eggs, room temperature
- 1 1/2 teaspoons baking powder
- 2 cups all purpose flour
- 3/4 cups whole milk

For the crunchy FILLING and TOPPING you will need:
- 3/4 cup all purpose flour
- 1/4 cup sugar
- 1 tablespoon corn starch
- 3 tablespoons cocoa powder
- 1/4 cup butter

For the ICING, you will need:
- 1 1/4 cups cream cheese
- 1/2 cup butter, room temperature
- 1/2 cup smooth peanut butter
- 1 teaspoon vanilla extract
- 3 1/2 cups powdered sugar
- 2-3 tablespoons milk

STEPS TO COOK

01. Preheat the oven to 350 degrees.
02. Cream together butter and sugar until light and fluffy, this may take several minutes. Add peanut butter and vanilla, mix until smooth. Add eggs, one at a time, mixing after each until combined. If your mixture looks curdled, this is normal. Don't panic! Scrape down the sides of the mixing bowl. Add baking powder and half of the flour, mix until just combined. Add remaining flour.
Blend until smooth, but don't over mix the batter. Pour into pans.

SUGGESTED PAN SIZE:
This cake recipe calls for two 9" round cake pans. Bake for 25-30 minutes.

TO MAKE THE CRUNCHY FILLING AND TOPPING:
01. In a large mixing bowl, add plain flour, sugar, corn-flour and cocoa powder. Whisk together. Melt your butter and add it to the mixture, stirring until it forms wet crumbs. Pour this mixture out onto a baking tray lined with baking paper and spread out into one layer. Bake for 10 minutes, then leave to cool completely.

TO MAKE THE ICING:
01. In a bowl, combine cream cheese and butter. Beat until light and fluffy. Add peanut butter and vanilla, blend until smooth. Add powdered sugar, one cup at a time, along with milk, mixing well. If the frosting is too thick, add additional tablespoon of milk.

Apply icing to the cake once it is cool. Sprinkle a layer of the crunchy cookie filling. Feel free to be creative with the décor of this cake!!

It can be iced in a naked cake presentation as well.

There's a photo of the fluffy version, and another photo with the girls, of the naked version.

Cake can be stored in a container in the refrigerator for up to three days. This cake is typically gone before then!

The three girls in this picture LOVE them some peanut butter, and they loved this peanut butter cake!! They're all incredibly different. The hair color gives you the first clue, doesn't it? Their personalities are nothing alike, their likes and dislikes are clearly different. But the piece of me that's visible is the same. They're confident, opinionated, and they LOVE a sweet if it contains peanut butter!!

These girls have so much more figured out than I did at this age. To GOD be the glory!! I love their honesty, their wit, and their hearts!

They teach me daily that presentation is the key. Authenticity is a basic quality for me, but they remind me to present my brand of authenticity with an attempt at eye appeal. Ha!! In other words, put some paint on the old barn, Granny!!

Granddaughters keep us in line on make-up, fashion, and many things!! We are a family of honest women, and these three are prime examples.

And here's the best little peanut butter cake on planet earth, with the smartest, prettiest, twenty-something year-olds in Tennessee, ready to DEVOUR said cake!!!!!

And I say, "LET THEM EAT CAKE!!!!" Always and forever!!!!!!

CHOCOLATE SKILLET CAKE

INGREDIENTS

For the CAKE, you will need:
- 1 cup of flour
- 1/2 teaspoon of baking soda
- 1 cup of sugar
- Dash of salt
- 1/4 cup of butter, softened
- 1/4 cup of vegetable oil
- 2 tablespoons cocoa powder
- 1/2 cup of water
- 1/4 cup of buttermilk
- 1 egg
- 1/2 teaspoon vanilla

For the ICING, you will need:
- 1/4 cup of butter
- 2 tablespoons of cocoa
- 3-4 tablespoons of milk
- 1/2 cup of chopped pecans
- 2 cups of powdered sugar
- 1/2 teaspoon vanilla

You MAY need:
- Ice Cream for serving. A good vanilla works perfectly, however you can use any of your favorite flavors! Be creative.
- Caramel or Fudge sauce for serving.
- Whipped cream for serving.

STEPS TO COOK

01. Preheat the oven to 350 degrees.
02. In a bowl, whisk together flour, baking soda, sugar and salt and set aside. In your cast iron skillet bring the butter, oil, cocoa powder, and water to a boil. Remove it from the heat and whisk in the dry ingredients. Mix in the buttermilk, egg and vanilla. Blend until smooth, but don't over mix the batter.

<u>**SUGGESTED PAN SIZE**</u>:
This cake recipe calls for a 10" cast iron skillet. Bake for 15-20 minutes.

<u>**TO MAKE THE ICING:**</u>
You will want to make the icing while the cake is beginning to cool.

01. In a saucepan bring the butter, cocoa and milk to a boil. Remove them from heat and add the sugar, nuts and vanilla. Stir until combined.

Pour icing over warm cake. Spread until the cake is evenly covered.

Serve warm with ice cream, sauce and whipped cream!

Well, here we go again!! Chocolate!!! A skillet!! And a heavenly dessert made with Cocoa!!
My friend Barbara sent me this cake. She's such a neat lady. She can cook like a master chef, loves like Jesus, and her super power? She has LOVED, and served my kiddos for twenty-five years!! No, she's not an employee. She's one of those "road moms." For those of you who live in a cave, and may not know our history, here's the scoop.

We traveled as a family for many years. The kids sang, minus Krystal, who stayed behind and ran the office. The bus would pull into town, maybe one of us needed a run to Walmart, or Walgreen's for medicine, or maybe it was as simple as we needed a large safety pin. We always had our people. People who we didn't mind seeing our messy bus, our housecoat and flip-flops.

About twenty years ago, I had to leave the road. Suddenly, not my decision, but nevertheless, leave I did. We do what we have to do. So people like Barbara became my proxy. Kind folks, all over the country, would run to the nearest store to bring ice when the bus air wasn't working, they would stock the kids up on whatever there was need of.

And Barbara is more than a friend. She's cut of the same cloth I am. She loves a GOOD CAKE!!And she's never steered me wrong on a recipe!!! And Lord have mercy, this one is a MUST try.

Plan to make this one, invite people over at a specific time. You truly need to serve this warm!!!

THREE STRANDS ULTIMATE CHOCOLATE CAKE

This recipe is for the SERIOUS chocolate lover!

INGREDIENTS

For the CAKE, you will need:
- 2 cups sugar
- 1 cup butter softened
- 1 1/2 teaspoons pure vanilla extract
- 3 large eggs
- 2 1/2 cups cake flour (Don't have cake flour? You can make your own by sifting together all purpose bleached flour and cornstarch. 3/4 cup of flour plus 2 tablespoons of starch per cup of cake flour called for!)
- 1 cup baking cocoa sifted
- 2 teaspoons baking soda
- 1/2 teaspoon salt
- 1/2 cup instant chocolate pudding mix (small box)
- 2 cups buttermilk
- ¼ cup strong black coffee, cooled
- 1 cup semi-sweet chocolate chips

For the ICING, you will need:
- 1/2 cup water
- 1/2 cup butter
- 1 teaspoon vanilla
- 1 cup baking cocoa sifted
- 3 1/2 cups powdered sugar
- 3 tablespoons heavy cream (more or less for consistency)

STEPS TO COOK

01. Preheat CONVECTION oven to 350 degrees.
02. Beat sugar, butter & vanilla in large bowl. Beat in eggs.
    - Mix in cake flour, baking cocoa, soda, salt, chocolate pudding mix, buttermilk and coffee. Stir in semi-sweet chocolate chips.
    - Pour into greased pan.
    - Cool cake completely before icing.
    - Blend until smooth, but don't over mix the batter. Pour into pans.

SUGGESTED PAN SIZE:
This cake recipe calls for a greased and floured tube or large bundt pan.
For a CONVECTION oven bake at 350 for approximately 60-70 minutes.

For a CONVENTIONAL oven bake at 350° for 30 minutes. Adjust baking temperature down to 325° and continue baking 30-40 minutes more, until cake tester comes out clean.(Check with cake tester at the one hour mark.)

TO MAKE THE ICING:
01. Heat water, butter and vanilla together in sauce pan on stove top until melted. Remove from heat. Stir in one cup cocoa. Stir in powdered sugar, sifted.
02. Stir in heavy cream, up to 3 tablespoons until you get the desired consistency.

Ice cake by filling the hole in the middle of the cake first, then spread icing over the cake and pour over the sides. Icing will harden as it cools.

Krystal makes this cake, and it's a favorite. The level of euphoria that I feel when I eat an icing with cocoa powder as a part of the ingredient, it's almost too much for me. Heaven comes down for about 45 seconds. But then? I usually have heart palpitations!! Ha!! Old people problems. I am a sucker for cocoa anything.

Which makes me think of a grandkid incident. You probably had to be there. But I will attempt to explain!

This "you had to be there" story happened about twelve or fourteen years ago, if memory serves me. I had a large walk in pantry at my old house on Riva Ridge. It was a room. The grandkids would go in there and play, and it often led to mayhem. Sprinkles everywhere, chips, cookies, what have you. There was a dozen of them, and they were quite the crew when they were little.

Hope and Cameron told Katelanne that cocoa was yummy, and SHE SHOULD have a big tablespoon for dessert!! Well, that baby was about two, and she took the bait. She put that heaping tablespoon of cocoa in her mouth? And it was katy-bar-the-door!! She threw the box, busted through that door, and ran to the bathroom...AND threw up. Crying, choking, and screaming at her sister all the WAY THERE!!!

I was finding cocoa powder in cracks a year later!!! The fine dusting of cocoa is not what you want flung in your pantry!! And they still tell the story, and I still remember the cloud of Cocoa like it was yesterday.

The lesson here? Eat Cocoa, but don't throw it!! Ha!!

This cake is CRAZY good. Honestly, it will almost change your life!! Make it and wait for a little bit of Heaven to come down!

THE HUMBLE POTATO CAKE

INGREDIENTS

For the POTATO CAKE, you will need:
- 5 medium baking potatoes
- 3 tablespoon butter
- 2 teaspoon salt
- 2 teaspoon black pepper
- 3 tablespoons cooking oil
- 1 clove garlic, minced
- 5 scallions, finely copped

STEPS TO COOK

01. I suggest an iron skillet, as usual!! Rinse and peel potatoes, and soak for 30 minutes if you have the time. If not, no big deal. Slice thinly, preferably with a slicer.

02. Melt butter in a large skillet over low heat and sauté garlic for 1-2 minutes, or until fragrant.

03. Remove potatoes from water and pat dry with a paper towel.

04. Place dry potatoes in a large bowl and pour 3/4 garlic butter over them, reserving the rest for later use. Season generously with salt and pepper and toss until everything is evenly coated.

05. Add oil to the skillet and heat until it's shimmering and ripply. Remove pan from heat and add potatoes in a spiral formation; adding a few scallions to every layer. Remember that the potatoes on the bottom of the skillet will be the top of the "cake."

    Once all the slices are in the pan, press it flat like a cake.

06. Bake for 35-45 minutes, or until tender. Lift edges of cake and check that it is browned; potatoes should be fork tender. Invert cake onto a large plate.

07. Cut cake into wedges and serve hot.

The ingredient list probably doesn't require a trip to the grocery. But, this recipe can be a bit labor intensive, especially if you don't have a slicer. But we all know that potatoes are truly the star of many meals, and this is something that you need to try!! This dish forms a crispy crust on the outside when it's cooked a bit longer than is recommended!! And I LOVE that. It reminds me of Momma's fried potatoes.

So, this is the 2020 spin on an old favorite!! You won't be disappointed. Grab the skillet and do this!!

Personally, I've never met a potato I didn't like. How about you? When deciding to choose my final savory cake, there are only four in this book, I knew that I had to do this one!!

As I gush over recipes, look forward to making them...always, I am keenly aware that ten percent of the world will go to bed with less nutrition than needed tonight. 815 million people are undernourished or hungry, worldwide, in 2020.

This chubby girl struggles with living in a world where third world countries are so corrupt that the people never get the intended food. I struggle with lots of things. And this isn't the place to sprinkle guilt or sadness. This is a happy book!! We're going to make potatoes and enjoy them.

However, 2020 left a mark on me. During this horrible pandemic, we raised the money, and fed thousands. That's such a big part of my heart. My red-haired granddaughter Eden...volunteered to help me. She said, "Granny, I have a phone. I can order groceries while I take care of my girls and husband." And she did, we did, you did!! Eden became an online grocery-shopping expert, overnight. My friend Dawn became a delivery expert. It was AMAZING to watch!!

We had a grocery army that delivered groceries all over the continental United States!! MANY bags of yummy potatoes were in those deliveries.

So what's my point?? I want to speak to you for one minute about what WE can do, even now. If in doubt? Feed them. If you know a little elderly woman, take her a bag of groceries once a month. Find out what she likes, eats, needs. You can have groceries delivered in many areas these days. Make it a recurring gift.

Or, if you know a single mom who works tirelessly to make ends meet, yet it's nearly impossible for the math to work. There's never enough money to buy what her family needs. Again. A bag of groceries, once a month. God will be pleased, and so will you. Giving feels better than getting. Try it!!

And oh yeah, make this little potato cake for your family!! It's simply divine.

BRIAN'S AMAZING ECLAIR "CAKE"

This is a simple "cake" that our family loves! It is easy to make and does not require an oven, making it a favorite.

INGREDIENTS

For the CAKE, you will need:
- 1 box of graham crackers
- 2 small boxes of vanilla instant pudding mix
- 3 cups of milk
- 1 container of Cool Whip topping, thawed

For the ICING, you will need:
- 1 container your favorite chocolate or fudge icing

STEPS TO COOK

01. Line the bottom of your pan with graham crackers.

02. Combine the pudding mix and milk in a bowl, whisking until combined. Scrape the sides and bottom of the bowl. Mix in the thawed whipped topping, until combined. Layer half of the pudding mixture on top of graham crackers, spreading evenly. Add another layer of graham crackers and pudding mix, finishing with a third layer of graham crackers. Cover the pan with plastic wrap and place in the refrigerator to firm up, about one hour.

SUGGESTED PAN SIZE:

This cake recipe calls for a 9" x 13" pan.

TO MAKE THE ICING:

01. Warm the icing for 30 seconds in the microwave and stir. Heat for an additional 15-30 seconds if needed. You want the icing to be pourable.

02. Apply icing to the cake once it is firm. Cover and place back into the refrigerator for an additional 4 hours before serving. This cake can be made up to one day prior to serving.

VARIATIONS:

You can use any flavor pudding mix that you desire. French vanilla, cheesecake, white chocolate, even banana, they all make a great dessert! This gets better as it sits for a day or two….. if it lasts that long.

Krystal and Brian do a lot of entertaining, church folks, friends, and of course family. Brian is from North Carolina, and of course we're form Kentucky!! Krystal eats mutton (we're from western Kentucky where it's common) and he hates it. He eats liver-mush (a gross concoction that he swears is good) and I think she hates that!! Our Kentucky deviled eggs are sweet, and contain sweet pickle juice, and the grandkids LOVE them. The North Carolina version, that he makes, aren't sweet at all. I will eat them, but I can't quite understand them. Not a sign of sugar or sweet pickles. Why?? Just why would you waste an egg on this!! Ha!! Krystal loves old fashioned Kentucky vegetable soup made with ground beef, and he hates it. You get the picture. Ha!!

Have you ever stopped and thought about the regional food likes and dislikes that are baked into the cake, no pun intended, with our likes and dislikes? We develop our likes and dislikes very early in life. New Orleans folk love crawfish. They ain't scared. They feeding their babies crawfish etouffee before they can walk!!! But there are areas of the country that you would be hard pressed to find people who eat crawfish. And yes, the same with mutton. My girls eat it, because I served it when they were little. But I don't think Terah, Adam, Aaron, or Jason care for it, nor the in-laws. I got them a little later in life. They missed out on developing a like for the strong taste of a barbecue mutton sandwich. You either love it, or you hate it. And I love it!!

Back to Brian and Krystal. There were definitely food differences to be dealt with when they decided to marry and form a cooking union, because they booth cook! A lot!! And both are great cooks!!

And they're both foodies. Honestly, I don't know anyone that's more interested in recipes and new restaurants than these two!! If you want to know where to eat when in Nashville? I ain't your girl. Ask them!!

So, when Brian told me his recipe is easy and book worthy, I believed him. Brian started making this for the kids, years ago. And yes, they ask for it for their birthdays sometimes. That means it's five stars, and highly recommended.

So, we may not agree on deviled eggs or liver-mush, but we're always in TOTAL lockstep on cakes. Well, unless they contain coffee. I HATE coffee. That's another story, another day!!

Make this cake and enjoy it!! You didn't even have to turn the oven on. That's the perfect dessert!!

Notes:

www.kathycrabbhannah.com

Notes:

Kathy's Cakebook

Follow me on Facebook and Instagram
Kathy Crabb Hannah   kathycrabbhannah